Target 5
Get back on track

AQA GCSE (9–1)
Spanish
Reading

Viv Halksworth

Published by Pearson Education Limited, 80 Strand, London, WC2R 0RL

www.pearsonschoolsandfecolleges.co.uk

Text © Pearson Education Ltd 2018
Produced by Out of House Publishing
Typeset by Newgen KnowledgeWorks Pvt. Ltd., Chennai, India

The right of Viv Halksworth to be identified as the author of this work has been asserted by her in accordance with the Copyright, Designs and Patents Act 1988.

First published 2018

21 20 19 18
10 9 8 7 6 5 4 3 2 1

British Library Cataloguing in Publication Data
A catalogue record for this book is available from the British Library.

ISBN 978 0435 18911 2

Printed in Slovakia by Neografia

Acknowledgments
p19 Lindo, Elvira; Manolito Gafotas; © 1994 Seix Barral

Note from the publisher
Pearson has robust editorial processes, including answer and fact checks, to ensure the accuracy of the content in this publication, and every effort is made to ensure this publication is free of errors. We are, however, only human, and occasionally errors do occur. Pearson is not liable for any misunderstandings that arise as a result of errors in this publication, but it is our priority to ensure that the content is accurate. If you spot an error, please do contact us at resourcescorrections@pearson.com so we can make sure it is corrected.

This workbook has been developed using the Pearson Progression Map and Scale for Spanish.

To find out more about the Progression Scale for Spanish and to see how it relates to indicative GCSE 9–1 grades go to www.pearsonschools.co.uk/ProgressionServices

Helping you to formulate grade predictions, apply interventions and track progress.

Any reference to indicative grades in the pearson Target Workbooks and Pearson Progression Services is not to be used as an accurate indicator of how a student will be awarded a grade for their GCSE exams.

You have told us that mapping the Steps from the Pearson Progression Maps to indicative grades will make it simpler for you to accumulate the evidence to formulate your own grade predictions, apply any interventions and track student progress. We're really excited about this work and its potential for helping teachers and students. It is, however, important to understand that this mapping is for guidance only to support teachers' own predictions of progress and is not an accurate predictor of grades.

Our Pearson Progression Scale is criterion referenced. If a student can perform a task or demonstrate a skill, we say they are working at a certain Step according to the criteria. Teachers can mark assessments and issue results with reference to these criteria which do not depend on the wider cohort in any given year. For GCSE exams however, all Awarding Organisations set the grade boundaries with reference to the strength of the cohort in any given year. For more information about how this works please visit: https://www.gov.uk/government/news/setting-standards-for-new-gcses-in-2017

Contents

(1) Recognising and understanding core vocabulary

This unit will help you to learn how to recognise and understand the vocabulary that you need to answer the question. The skills that you will build are to:

- recognise common words
- show understanding of common words once you have recognised them
- take account of the context when showing understanding of common words.

In the exam, you will be asked to do reading tasks similar to the ones on these two pages. This unit will prepare you to tackle these questions and choose or come up with the best answers.

(1) For this exam task you first need to identify vocabulary for expressing opinions. Circle (A) the nine words and phrases that introduce an opinion.

Do not answer this question yet. You will be asked to come back to it at the end of the unit.

Exam-style question

Viajes y turismo

Lee estas opiniones en una página web sobre las vacaciones. *holidays*

Prefiero pasar las vacaciones en la costa, porque me encanta tomar el sol y nadar en el mar. Lo más importante es relajarme.	*Miguel*
Me gustan los hoteles cómodos, de cinco estrellas, con una variedad de tiendas y restaurantes y con aire acondicionado. No me interesa hacer camping.	*Susana*
Me encanta ir al extranjero. Saco fotos y como la cocina tradicional. Me fascinan las fiestas tradicionales en los pueblos.	*Juan*
Para mí es importante estar al aire libre y ser activa. Es divertido montar a caballo y hacer esquí acuático.	*Amelia*

¿Qué tipo de vacaciones prefiere cada persona?

A	culturales
B	de sol y playa
C	lujosas
D	un crucero
E	deportivas
F	de invierno

1	Miguel	B	(1 mark)
2	Susana	C	(1 mark)
3	Juan	A	(1 mark)
4	Amelia	E	(1 mark)

---

(2) Scan the holiday plans below. Underline (A) the three places and circle (A) the four activities mentioned in the text.

To answer this question, it's important not just to recognise the words for places, but also to understand the words for activities to do with those places.

Do not answer this question yet. You will be asked to come back to it at the end of the unit.

Exam-style question

Vacaciones

Lees este correo electrónico de Antonio con sus planes para mañana.

> Planes para mañana
>
> 1 – al castillo y el puente romano _roman bridge_
> 2 – comprar comida para la merienda en la playa _tea_
> 3 – tomar un refresco después de tomar el sol _to Drink Soda after to sunbathe_
> 4 – comprar regalos para la familia _Presents_

¿Dónde va a hacer Antonio cada una de las actividades?

A	café
B	hotel
C	monumentos
D	museo
E	centro de ocio
F	supermercado
G	tienda de regalos

Escribe la letra correcta en cada casilla.

Plan 1   C   (1 mark)

Plan 2   A   (1 mark)

Plan 3   B   (1 mark)

Plan 4   G   (1 mark)

The three key questions in the **skills boosts** will help you improve how you answer these types of questions.

1 How do I recognise common words?

2 How do I show understanding of common words once I have recognised them?

3 How do I take account of the context when showing understanding of common words?

1 How do I recognise common words?

It's a good idea to learn words in blocks related to topic areas. It also helps to associate nouns with certain verbs. That way, when you read an exam text, you will be able to recognise and understand words in relation to each other.

1 a Look at this list of holiday vocabulary. Match ✐ the Spanish to the English words by writing the letters in the boxes.

A rent	B souvenirs	C car	D youth hostel	E lose	F buy
G stay	H plane	I travel	J castle	K visit	L luggage

i albergue juvenil	D	v viajar	I	ix alquilar	A
ii avión	H	vi comprar	F	x coche	C
iii visitar	K	vii castillo	J	xi equipaje	L
iv recuerdos	B	viii alojarse	G	xii perder	E

b Now look at these words from **a**. Choose other words from the list above and write ✐ pairs of related words: one noun and one verb in each pair. Use this technique to learn vocabulary in different topic groups.

Example: albergue juvenil _alojarse_

i avión _Viajar_

ii visitar _Castillo_

iii recuerdos _Comprar_

iv alquilar _albergue Juvenil_

v equipaje _perder_

> Remember that different words may be used to express the same thing. Think of **related vocabulary** to help you answer the question (e.g. _dinero: el precio, el coste, caro, barato, la tarjeta de crédito, el banco, costar_).
>
> To help you learn vocabulary you can also try grouping words with the **same stem** (_el alojamiento – alojarse, la visita – visitar_) or with their _opposites_ (_caro – barato, frío – calor_).

2 Look at the statements (A–F) and the questions (i-iv) below.

A	Viajo en tren porque tengo miedo de volar. Además, me gusta ver el paisaje.	Ana
B	Quiero reservar una habitación con vistas al mar y media pensión.	Bernardo
C	Me gustaría ir de vacaciones con mis amigos porque sería muy divertido.	Carmen
D	Prefiero alojarme en un camping porque es más barato que un hotel.	David
E	No me importa el frío. Me encanta la nieve y quiero aprender a esquiar.	Elisa
F	Tengo que comprar una tienda nueva y un saco de dormir.	Federico

i Who is careful with money? `D`

ii Who doesn't like planes? `A`

iii Who would like a winter holiday? `E`

iv Who wants a change from holidays with parents? `C`

a Circle Ⓐ the key words in the Spanish statements (A–F) which relate to each of the questions in English (i-iv).

b Who says what? Write ✐ the correct letter (A–F) in the boxes after each of the questions (i-iv).

2 **How do I show understanding of common words once I have recognised them?**

Reading the texts and questions carefully and using your knowledge of common words will help you find the right answer.

1 **a** Read the Spanish and English sentences in **b** and **c**, respectively. The key words in **c** are all places in a town. In the Spanish sentences, highlight the key words related to those places.

b Annotate the Spanish key words to show how they relate to a place.

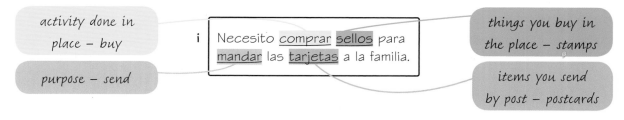

activity done in place – buy

purpose – send

i Necesito comprar sellos para mandar las tarjetas a la familia.

things you buy in the place – stamps

items you send by post – postcards

ii | Esta tarde vamos al partido y antes tengo que comprar las entradas.

iii | Tengo que comprar crema solar para ir a la playa porque no quiero quemarme.

iv | Primero pierdo el pasaporte y luego pierdo la cartera. ¡Qué desastre!

v | Mi alojamiento tiene una piscina climatizada y dos restaurantes.

vi | Necesito un plan del pueblo y un folleto sobre los lugares de interés.

Use the words that you are familiar with to help you understand the gist of the text and you'll find that unfamiliar words won't affect your answer. You may even be able to guess their meaning by placing them in context.

c Now write the letter for the correct Spanish sentence in **b** for each English statement.

A I want to go to the chemist.    iii

B I'm going to the stadium later today.   ii

C I need to find a post office.   i

D I'm looking for a tourist information office.   vi

E Is there a police station nearby?   iv

F I'm staying at a nice hotel.   v

3 **How do I take account of the context when showing understanding of common words?**

When reading a Spanish text use grammatical clues to help you understand a word in context and answer a question.

> Prepositions can alter the meaning of a sentence and they can mean different things in different contexts.
> a = to, at   por = through, for, to, by
> de = of, from   para = in order to, for
> en = in, on, at

① **a** Read the sentences. In each case, decide what the preposition means and circle Ⓐ the correct answer.

Example:

A | Ricardo vuelve **a** la oficina. | (to)/ at   B | Ricardo vuelve **a** las ocho. | to /(at)

train

i   A | El tren sale **para** Madrid. | to /(for)   B | Voy a la playa **para** nadar. | (to)/ for

ii A | El autocar pasa **por** Francia. | B | Quiero una canción hecha **por** Shakira. |
through / by   through /(by)

iii A | El museo está abierto **de** las nueve a las seis. | B | Quiero una lista **de** sitios de interés. |
of / from   (of)/ from

iv A | El bañador está **en** la maleta. | (in)/ on   B | El libro está **en** la mesa. | in /(on)

b On paper, write ✏ how you worked out the correct meaning of the prepositions in **a**.

Example: *Sentence A says 'returns' and 'office' so 'a' must mean 'to'. In sentence B 'a las ocho' is time so 'a' must mean 'at'.*

② Read the English sentences and choose the phrase in Spanish that best conveys the meaning. Highlight ✏ and annotate ✏ the Spanish sentences to help you work out the correct answer.

Example: I go to the post office to post my cards. *ii*

i Voy a mandar **las tarjetas** por correo.   ii Voy **a correos** a **mandar** las tarjetas.

Immediate future tense   'by'   *post*   *Present tense*   *preposition '(in order) to'*   *postcards*

a I'm attending a sailing club for beginners. .....ii.....

i Lo principal es empezar una clase de vela.   ii Asisto a una clase de vela para principiantes.

b The plane is delayed by an hour. .....i.....

i El avión lleva una hora de retraso.   ii No sé a qué hora llega el avión.

c I love Spanish cooking. .....i.....

i Me apasiona la cocina española.   ii Le entusiasma la cocina española.

d All the rooms have new hair dryers. .....ii.....

i Hay un secador nuevo en mi habitación.   ii Todas las habitaciones tienen secadores nuevos.

Your turn!

Here is an exam-style question which requires you to put into practice the skills you have worked on, especially showing understanding of common words once you have recognised them. ✏

Exam-style question

Local area holidays and travel

Read what these people say about their holiday activities on a website forum.

A	Para mí, lo importante es ver lo típico de un país. Cuando voy al extranjero me gusta probar los platos de la región.	Ángela
B	Lo bueno de las vacaciones es tener tiempo para leer. Me encanta tumbarme al sol al lado de la piscina con una buena novela.	Barnabás
C	Lo que me chifla es la vida nocturna. No me interesan los monumentos y las cosas antiguas. Quiero bailar y pasarlo bien en las fiestas.	Carlota
D	Paso el mes de agosto en el pueblo donde viven mis abuelos. Es divertido ir en bici al río con mis primos y pescar.	Daniel
E	Me fascina la vida del pasado y por eso siempre visito los museos y los castillos. Los edificios viejos son muy interesantes.	Elena
F	Para mí es esencial probar algo nuevo y emocionante como un deporte acuático o una nueva aventura.	Fernando
G	Siempre voy a la costa porque busco oportunidades de hacer excursiones en barco o practicar windsurf.	Susana

Who says what about their holiday activities?

Example: Who enjoys sunbathing? | B |

1   Who samples the local food? | A | (1 mark)

2   Who enjoys spending time with the family? | D | (1 mark)

3   Who likes historical monuments? | E | (1 mark)

4   Who prefers going out at night? | C | (1 mark)

> Rather than looking for direct translations of the questions in English, find vocabulary associated with the key words. For example, in the forum Barnabás doesn't directly say he enjoys sunbathing, but he does use the words 'me encanta tumbarme al sol' which implies that he does. You may not recognise the verb 'tumbarse', but the fact that he's in the sun, by a pool and not doing anything else but reading suggests that he enjoys sunbathing.

Your turn!

Here is an exam style question which requires you to put into practice the skills you have worked on, specifically recognising and understanding words in relation to each other. ✎

Exam-style question

Holidays

You read Mariela's email telling you about her day.

> ¡Hola!
>
> Primero hice footing en el parque antes de llevar el coche a arreglar. Fui de compras a por un bañador nuevo y sandalias para el verano. Compré un bocadillo y fruta para comer más tarde.
>
> Luego, alquilé una bici para dar un paseo por el río. Visité el museo después de comer en el parque. Después de devolver la bici, recogí el coche y pagué al mecánico.

A	gym
B	supermarket
C	museum
D	park

E	clothes shop
F	garage
G	bike hire shop
H	restaurant

Where did Mariela go? Complete each sentence.

Write the correct letter in each box.

Example: Before taking her car to be fixed, Mariela went to the ...   [D]

1 To be ready for her summer holiday Mariela needed to go to the ...   [E]   (1 mark)

2 To buy her lunch she went to the ...   [B]   (1 mark)

3 Before going cycling she went to the ...   G [F]   (1 mark)

4 After lunch she went to the ...   [C]   (1 mark)

5 Finally, she went to the ...   F [G]   (1 mark)

When reading the text, look out for prepositions such as *por, para, de* and *a*, which might indicate why someone did something.

Read the parts of the question carefully, looking out for words like 'before, after, finally' that signal where to find the information in the text.

Review your skills

Check up

Review your responses to the exam-style questions on pages 7 and 8. Tick ✓ the column that shows how well you think you have done each of the following.

	Not quite ✓	Nearly there ✓	Got it! ✓
recognised common words	☐	✓	☐
shown understanding of common words once I have recognised them	☐	☐	✓
taken account of context when showing understanding of common words	☐	✓	☐

Need more practice?

Go back to pages 2 and 3 and complete 🖉 the two exam-style questions there. Use the checklist to help you.

Checklist In my answers, do I...	✓
identify and understand words from the topic lists?	
not distort my answer by guessing the meaning of unfamiliar words?	
use grammatical clues to work out my answer?	

Learn words in relation to each other. Group them into topics and then sub group them again into topic areas, e.g. holidays: types of holiday, activities, weather, transport, places, accommodation, clothes, problems, etc. You could make mind maps to help you remember the words.

How confident do you feel about each of these **skills**? Colour in 🖉 the bars.

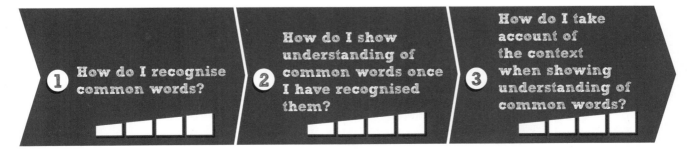

1 How do I recognise common words?

2 How do I show understanding of common words once I have recognised them?

3 How do I take account of the context when showing understanding of common words?

② Recognising cognates and near-cognates

This unit will help you learn how to use cognates and near-cognates to make sense of texts. The skills you will build are to:

- recognise and understand cognates (words that look and mean the same in both languages)
- recognise and understand near-cognates (words that look similar but whose forms or endings might be different)
- identify and be careful of 'false friends', words that look the same or similar in both languages but mean something different.

In the exam, you will be asked to tackle reading tasks such as the ones on these two pages. This unit will prepare you to understand different styles of texts, including newspaper articles.

Do not answer this question yet. You will be asked to come back to it at the end of the unit.

Exam-style question

School problems

You see this article about bullying in a Spanish newspaper.

> Un estudio del Ministerio de Educación sobre el acoso escolar concluye que la intimidación en las redes sociales representa uno de cada cuatro casos de acoso escolar en España. Sin embargo, a partir de los 13 años, el 36,5% de los casos de acoso son por ciberacoso. Otra conclusión es que el 70% de las víctimas de ciberacoso son chicas.
>
> _one in every four_ (handwritten annotation)
>
> El silencio ya no es una constante en los casos de acoso escolar. Ni por parte de las víctimas ni de sus compañeros. Más de la mitad de los estudiantes intimidados acusan a los agresores. Además, los profesores cada vez son más conscientes de lo que ocurre dentro y fuera del aula y el patio.
>
> _teacher are extreamly aware_ (handwritten annotation)

Answer the following questions **in English**.

1 Overall, how much bullying takes place in Spain through social media?

   One in every four (handwritten answer)   (1 mark)

2 Who are the main victims of cyberbullying?

   Main victims are girls (handwritten answer)   (1 mark)

3 How have attitudes to bullying changed? Mention **one** thing.

   teacher are extreamly aware (handwritten answer)   (1 mark)

---

(1) Skim through the blog below and underline (A) at least 10 words that look like English. Highlight 🖉 any false friends.

> Understanding a text can sometimes hang on the meaning of one word in a sentence. If that word is a cognate or a near-cognate, it can help you. If it is a 'false friend', it can lead to errors so beware!

Do not answer this question yet. You will be asked to come back to it at the end of the unit.

Exam-style question

The good and bad things about school

You read Carmela's blog about her school on a Cuban website.

> Para mí, lo peor de mi instituto es que no hay instalaciones deportivas adecuadas como un gimnasio bien equipado. Como quiero estudiar ciencias deportivas en la universidad, esto es una frustración.
>
> Otro problema es que los laboratorios de ciencias son muy antiguos y por lo tanto no es fácil aprender en tales condiciones.
>
> Lo bueno de mi instituto son los profesores que son muy simpáticos, con la excepción del profesor de matemáticas, que es muy estricto. Mi profesora de español tiene muy buen sentido del humor y nos hace reír. Además, organiza excursiones extraescolares al cine a ver películas en español. De esa manera, nos divertimos aprendiendo.

Answer the following questions **in English**.

1   What is wrong with the sports' facilities in Carmela's school?

....It's Equipped.. (1 mark)

2   What does she want to study at university?

....Sports science.. (1 mark)

3   Why isn't it easy to study science at her school?

....because of the conditions............................... (1 mark)

4   Who is strict at Carmela's school?

....math teacher... (1 mark)

The three key questions in the **skills boosts** will help you to improve how you answer this style of questions.

1 How do I recognise and understand cognates?

2 How do I recognise and understand near-cognates?

3 How do I identify 'false friends'?

1   How do I recognise and understand cognates?

When reading a text which might appear difficult at first, always look out for words that are the same or similar in both languages. This can help you make sense of the text.

> Many English and Spanish words have Latin or Greek roots and the same meaning; these words are called **cognates**. The Spanish language borrows many English words and, vice versa, English borrows many Spanish words. By knowing a few simple cognate rules, you can work out the meaning of many words.

① Have a quick look at these blog entries about school life. How do they seem to you at first glance? Tick ⊘ a box.

Very easy to understand ☐   fairly easy ☐   quite difficult ☑   very difficult ☐

a Voy al club de judo los jueves. En mi opinión, participar en las competiciones nacionales es una parte importante de la actividad. Además, en noviembre gané un trofeo.

b El uniforme en mi instituto es muy formal. Pienso que limita la individualidad, pero es práctico. Además, así las diferencias económicas entre los estudiantes no son tan obvias.

c Creo que las normas en el instituto son necesarias. Por ejemplo, no se permite usar el móvil en clase y está prohibido ser agresivo o grosero. También hay que ser puntual.

② Now read the three blog entries in ① again and underline Ⓐ at least five words in each entry that look the same or similar and mean the same in Spanish and English.

③ **a** Read these sentences and highlight ✎ examples of words which demonstrate spelling differences.

   i   Esta es una foto de mis compañeros de gimnasia.

   ii   En la clase de geografía, estudiamos la contaminación y el reciclaje.

   iii   El jueves hicimos una excursión para ver el estadio de los Juegos Olímpicos.

   iv   Gané un trofeo de esquí cuando fuimos a España.

   v   Después de mucho estrés, aprobé el examen y me sentí fenomenal.

Common spelling changes between Spanish and English:

f- = ph-	física	physics / physical
es- = s-	especial	special
-ión = -ion	televisión	television
-i- = -y- (as a vowel)	bicicleta	bicycle

b Make a list of the words from **a** you have highlighted. Write ✎ the English spelling alongside them and learn them.

opinión	nacionales	individualidad	agresivo
actividad	actividad	práctico	
importante	formal	estudiantes	
competiciones	uniforme	clase	

2 How do I recognise and understand near-cognates?

There are thousands of words in Spanish which, although they are not exactly the same as in English, are easily understood if you are aware of some typical differences in spelling.

1 **a** Read these sentences and highlight 🖊 all the cognates or near-cognates you can find. Then write 🖊 in the box how many you found in each sentence.

i El profesor de educación física es estricto, no tiene paciencia, pero controla bien la clase. `6`

ii Tengo que admitir que me gusta estudiar historia y geografía. `3`

iii Normalmente voy al club de fotografía los lunes. `3`

iv Después de mi experiencia, no puedo decidir si voy a participar otra vez. `2`

v Desafortunadamente el uniforme de mi colegio en primaria era feo. `1`

vi Para hacer esta actividad es necesario poner atención y aprender el vocabulario. `4`

vii En mi instituto no hay mucha intimidación ni violencia entre los estudiantes. `4`

viii Tengo la oportunidad de participar en un intercambio y visitar a mi amigo español. `4`

ix Estoy estudiando para el examen de biología. Tengo que escribir sobre un experimento. `4`

x Mi compañero de universidad no es estúpido; es muy inteligente, pero es muy tímido. `3`

b Translate 🖊 the sentences from **a** on paper.

2 This table contains changes to word endings between Spanish and English. Fill it 🖊 with examples from sentences in **1**.

Spanish	English	Examples from sentences
Verbs ending in consonant, add -ar or -ir		controlar/control
-ar or -ir	-e	estudiar, participar, visitar
Nouns or adjectives ending in -encia	-ence	experiencia paciencia violencia
-ario	-ary	necesario vocabulario
-ción	-tion	educación atención intimidación
-dad	-ty	universidad actividad oportunidad
-ía/-ia/-ío/-io	-y	historia geografía paciencia fotografía experiencia necesario
Nouns and adjectives ending in consonant, add -o/a or -e		inteligente historia biología geografía física uniforme paciencia
Adverbs ending in -mente	-ly	desafortunadamente experimento normalmente
Verb forms ending in -ando or -iendo	-ing	estudiando estúpido

③ How do I identify 'false friends'?

If cognates and near-cognates are 'good friends' which can help you, you need to be aware of 'false friends', words which (although they look identical or similar in both languages) can mean something very different.

① **a** Read the sentences about school life. Then read the word-for-word translations below. You'll soon notice they don't make sense! Underline Ⓐ the 'false friends' in the Spanish text.

> Remember that word order in Spanish isn't always the same as in English. For example, adjectives follow nouns.

b Correct ✏ the translation with words that make sense in the context.

> i   En el concurso de gimnasia no tuve <u>éxito</u> y salí en <u>último</u> lugar.
>
> ii Mi amigo es una persona <u>sensible</u> y le <u>disgustan</u> las <u>discusiones</u> en el <u>patio</u>.
>
> iii La comida del instituto es bastante <u>sana</u>, pero las <u>sopas</u> son <u>saladas</u> y por lo tanto siempre bebo un <u>vaso</u> de agua.
>
> iv Mi profesora <u>envía</u> cartas a casa si no somos <u>educados</u>.
>
> v   No <u>recuerdo</u> dónde está la <u>parada</u> de autobús <u>escolar</u>.
>
> vi Voy a <u>realizar</u> una <u>encuesta</u> para ver cuántas personas <u>asisten</u> a los clubs extraescolares.

>   *wasn't successful*   *last*
> i   In the gymnastics competition I ~~didn't have an exit~~ and I came ~~out in ultimate place~~.
>
>   *sensitive*   *upset*   *arguments*   *playground*
> ii My friend is a ~~sensible~~ person and he is ~~disgusted~~ by ~~discussions~~ on the ~~patio~~.
>
>   *healthy*   *soups are salty*   *glass*
> iii The food at school is quite ~~sane~~, but the ~~soap is salad~~ and therefore I always drink a ~~vase~~
>
> of water.
>
>   *sends*   *are rude*
> iv My teacher ~~envies~~ letters home if we ~~aren't educated~~.
>
>   *remember*   *school*
> v   I don't ~~record~~ where the ~~parade of scholar~~ bus is.
>
>   *carry out a survey about*   *attend*
> vi I'm going to ~~realise an inquest to~~ see how many people ~~assist~~ in the extracurricular activities.

② Write ✏ the correct number i–x for the correct English translation for these common false friends.

> | i countryside/field | ii factory | iii to catch a cold | iv misfortune | vi current |
> |---|---|---|---|---|
> | vii relative | viii pregnant | ix firefighter | x to crash | |

a actual   <u>Current</u> VI   **d** campo   <u>Countryside</u> i   **g** una desgracia   misfortune iv

b fábrica   II factory   **e** constiparse   to catch a cold iii   **h** embarazada   Pregnant viii

c bombero   Firefighter   **f** chocar   <u>crash</u> x   **i** pariente   <u>relative</u> vii
               IX

Your turn!

Here is an exam-style question which requires you to put into practice the skills you have worked on, specifically how to use cognates and near-cognates to help you understand a text. ✎

Exam-style question

School clubs

You read this blog about the school clubs Jorge goes to.

> Me gusta cambiar de clubs y actividades extraescolares cada trimestre porque me gusta aprender cosas nuevas. Esta vez seré miembro de la orquesta. Llevo dos años aprendiendo a tocar la trompeta y ya estoy listo para tocar con otras personas. Además, creo que participar en un concierto es algo muy emocionante.
>
> Aparte de la música me encanta la natación. Voy a nadar los miércoles después de las clases, cuando vamos a la piscina del polideportivo municipal. El instructor tiene mucha confianza en nosotros y participamos en concursos nacionales. Ganar un trofeo es mi sueño, pero el problema es que entrenar requiere mucho tiempo.

Answer the following questions **in English**.

1   How often does Jorge change clubs?

.... (1 mark)

2   How long has he been playing the trumpet?

.... (1 mark)

3   What does he think he is ready for?

.... (1 mark)

4   What is Jorge's dream?

.... (1 mark)

Make use of cognates or near-cognates to understand the text. Here, in the context of school clubs, **orquesta** is likely to mean exactly the same as *orchestra*.

Beware of false friends! Does **listo** mean the same in both languages?

Your turn!

This is another exam-style question for you to try out the skills you have worked on in this unit, particularly using cognates, near-cognates, and spotting false friends. ✏

Exam-style question

Read Alfonso's blog about taking part in an exchange.

Hace poco estuve en Liverpool en un intercambio. Al principio, me disgustaba todo: el ritmo de vida, el hablar, los horarios de comer... Pero poco a poco empecé a acostumbrarme a las diferencias y por fin empecé a ver similitudes entre los dos países. Por ejemplo, la cosa que encontré más curiosa fue que los alumnos ingleses no pueden llevar su propia ropa al instituto. Sin embargo, en España también terminamos llevando el mismo uniforme: ¡vaqueros! Un intercambio es algo que recomiendo a cualquier estudiante de idiomas, no solo porque mejoras tus conocimientos del idioma, sino también porque aprendes mucho sobre la vida diaria y las costumbres de otro país y esto para mí fue lo más interesante.

Always be on the look-out for words that are going to help you make sense of the texts, such as cognates or near-cognates with their typical spelling changes. Also remember that some words, despite sharing the same or similar spelling in both languages, do not mean the same!

Answer the following questions **in English**.

1   How did Alfonso start to feel after a while?

....

.... (1 mark)

2   What did Alfonso find the most strange?

....

.... (1 mark)

3   Why does Alfonso think that exchanges are a valuable experience. Give **one** reason.

....

.... (1 mark)

Review your skills

Check up

Review your responses to the exam-style questions on pages 15 and 16. Tick ✓ the column that shows how well you think you have done each of the following.

	Not quite ✓	Nearly there ✓	Got it! ✓
recognised and understood cognates	☐	☐	☐
recognised and understood near-cognates	☐	☐	☐
identified "false friends"	☐	☐	☐

Need more practice?

Go back to pages 10 and 11 and complete ✐ the two exam-style questions there. Use the checklist to help you.

Checklist Before I answer, have I checked if ...	✓
there are any cognates in the text that can help me understand the text?	
there are words which I can easily understand if I adapt the spelling?	
there are false friends I need to be careful of?	

Remember to use your common sense when deciding whether a Spanish word that looks like an English word means the same or not. You need to make sure it fits the context.

How confident do you feel about each of these **skills**? Colour in ✐ the bars.

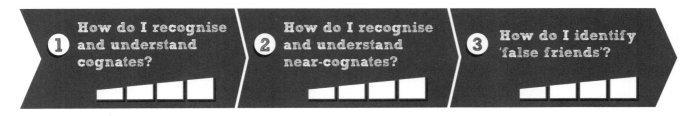

1 How do I recognise and understand cognates?

2 How do I recognise and understand near-cognates?

3 How do I identify 'false friends'?

3 Synonyms and antonyms

This unit will help you to answer the question by identifying words with similar and opposite meanings and from the topic they belong to. The skills you will build are to:

- recognise synonyms – words with similar meaning
- recognise antonyms – words with opposite meaning
- recognise words that belong to the same topic.

In the exam, you will be asked to do reading tasks similar to the ones on these two pages. This unit will prepare you to tackle these questions and choose or come up with the best answers.

Do not answer this question yet. You will be asked to come back to it at the end of the unit.

Exam-style question

Read Marisa's email.

Hola, Esteban.

Gracias por ayudarme a encontrar una familia inglesa para el intercambio. El año pasado estuve en un curso de verano y me quedé en casa de unos señores que eran bastante antipáticos, con niños traviesos y un perro muy desobediente. ¡No lo pasé bien!

Me gustaría estar en una familia más amable, que se lleva bien y con hijos simpáticos de mi edad. Tengo 16 años y soy activa, positiva y habladora. Me encanta practicar deportes, sobre todo la natación, el ciclismo y el atletismo. Prefiero estar al aire libre que en casa, pero también puedo divertirme con un buen libro o una película.

Mil gracias y hasta pronto:

Marisa

Write the correct letter in each box.

A	badly-behaved		D	kind		G	talkative
B	friend		E	reading		H	teenagers
C	funny		F	sport		I	unfriendly

1 What was the family that she stayed with last year like?   (1 mark)

2 What were their children and dog like?   (1 mark)

3 What does she hope the children will be this year?   (1 mark)

4 How does she describe herself?   (1 mark)

5 What is her favourite hobby?   (1 mark)

① Extracts from books, like the one below, are likely to have some words and phrases you don't know. But don't panic. Start by scanning the text for vocabulary you *do* know. What clues do they give you about where the characters are and what they are doing? Circle Ⓐ the words that help you decide.

Do not answer this question yet. You will be asked to come back to it at the end of the unit.

Exam-style question

Read this extract from *Manolito Gafotas* by Elvira Lindo.

Manolito and his father have just been to the opticians.

> Después del oculista fuimos a desayunar a una cafetería. Yo le dije a mi padre que quería sentarme en un taburete de los de la barra, de esos que dan vueltas. Molaba tres kilos. Mi padre me dejó pedir un batido, una palmera de chocolate y un donut. No había ningún otro niño en la cafetería. Me miré en el espejo de la cafetería para verme el peinado que me había hecho esa mañana y pensé: "A lo mejor creen que no soy un niño, a lo mejor piensan que en vez de ocho años tengo dieciocho. " (…) El camarero se acercó a mi padre y le dijo:
>
> – Parece que el niño tiene hambre – luego me dijo a mí –: Como sigas comiendo así te vas a hacer más alto que tu papá. –

Write the correct letter in each box.

Example: When is the story taking place?

A	in the morning
B	in the afternoon
C	in the evening

[*A*] (1 mark)

1 Where are Manolito and his father sitting?

A	at a table inside
B	at the bar
C	at a table outside

[   ] (1 mark)

2 What does Manolito have to drink?

A	coffee
B	milkshake
C	tea

[   ] (1 mark)

3 What does Manolito have to eat?

A	nothing
B	crisps
C	cakes

[   ] (1 mark)

4 What does Manolito notice about the other customers?

A	There are no other children.
B	There are several other children.
C	There is one other child.

[   ] (1 mark)

5 Who serves Manolito and his father?

A	a woman
B	a man
C	a girl

[   ] (1 mark)

The three key questions in the **skills boosts** will help you to improve how you answer this style of questions.

 ① How do I recognise synonyms?

 ② How do I recognise antonyms?

 ③ How do I recognise words that belong to the same topic?

How do I recognise synonyms?

> A **synonym** is a word that has the same meaning as another word. Some synonyms have the same roots, for example, *averiguar* and *verificar* from the Latin word 'veritas' (truth) and they mean 'to check that something is true'. But others don't look similar, for example, *acabar* and *terminar* (to finish).
>
> **Near-synonyms** have meanings which are similar rather than the same, for example, *simpático – amable, honrado – honesto, todos los días – cada día, malo – travieso, pasearse – dar una vuelta.*
>
> You may know more synonyms in Spanish than you think. The tasks on this page will help you to recognise and remember some of them.

① Choose the synonym from the list on the right and write ✐ it in the correct box.

Spanish	English	Spanish synonym
gratis	free	*gratuito*
a menudo	often	
desafortunadamente	unfortunately	
usar	to use	
dar una vuelta	to go for a walk	
divertido	amusing	
el ordenador	computer	
el teléfono	phone	
lo bueno de	the good thing about	
se puede	you can	

dar un paseo

desgraciadamente

el móvil

es posible

frecuentemente

~~gratuito~~

la ventaja de

el portátil

entretenido

utilizar

② Read the sentences. Underline Ⓐ eight words or phrases that you can replace with synonyms from ① and write ✐ them in the spaces. Change the verb and adjective forms where necessary.

Example: <u>La ventaja</u> de la tecnología móvil es que siempre estás en contacto con los amigos.

    Lo bueno de ....

ⓐ Se utilizan mucho las aplicaciones como WhatsApp e Instagram porque es gratuito mandar mensajes y fotos.

....

ⓑ Ahora se puede hacer casi todo en el teléfono, pero el portátil sirve mejor para hacer los deberes, ver videos y descargar música.

....

ⓒ Desgraciadamente hay mucho fraude en internet.

....

ⓓ Muchas veces los juegos que puedes jugar en los móviles son muy divertidos.

....

2   How do I recognise antonyms?

Words with opposite meanings are called **antonyms**. Recognising them can help you choose the correct answer for questions that don't use the same words as the text.

1   Sometimes antonyms are completely different words. Draw 🖉 lines to match the words into four pairs of antonyms:

A aburrido	a parecido
B bien	b menos
C distinto	c mal
D más	d divertido

> You can recognise some antonyms by their **prefixes** (the letters at the start of a word):
>
> simpático (nice, friendly)   **anti**pático (not nice, unfriendly)
> afortunadamente   **des**afortunadamente
> (fortunately)   (unfortunately)
> posible (possible)   **im**posible (impossible)
> soportable (bearable)   **in**soportable (unbearable)
> responsable (responsible)   **irr**esponsable (irresponsible)

2   Read what Marina says about her relationships with family and friends.

> Mi hermana y yo somos gemelas, pero somos distintas de carácter: ella es bastante callada y yo soy muy habladora. Nos peleamos de vez en cuando, pero normalmente nos llevamos bien porque compartimos las mismas aficiones.
>
> Mi amigo José y yo nos conocimos desde la escuela primaria y creo que nos llevamos bien porque somos muy distintos. Él es optimista mientras que yo suelo ser bastante pesimista.
>
> Mi madre y yo nos peleamos siempre. Para ella soy "imposible e inaguantable". Dice que soy irresponsable, pero creo que es ella quien tiene que ser menos impaciente. Sin embargo, me divierto mucho con mi padre y casi nunca discutimos. Es muy serio y responsable y mucha gente piensa, al principio, que es antipático, pero cuando lo conocen, se dan cuenta de que es paciente, simpático y generoso.

a   Find and circle Ⓐ the Spanish for the words in the box.

> chatty   we fight   optimistic   responsible   friendly   patient

b   Read the text again and underline Ⓐ the words that mean the opposite of the words you circled in **a**.

c   Read the text again. Which **four** statements about Marina are true? Use your work from **a** and **b** and your knowledge of antonyms to help you. Tick ✓ the correct letters.

A	She never argues with either of her parents.	
B	She usually gets on well with her sister.	
C	She has a very similar personality to her friend José.	
D	Her mother thinks she is unbearable.	
E	Her father can seem unfriendly at first.	
F	She has the same character as her twin.	
G	She met José in high school.	
H	She thinks her mother is impatient.	

3 **How do I recognise words that belong to the same topic?**

Learning words in **topic groups** makes it easier to remember them. Recognising which topic group a word belongs to can help you remember its meaning.

1 **a** Read the texts. Select and write 🖉 the topic group for each text from the box.

> Creo que las biografías son interesantes, pero las encuentro bastante serias. Me chiflan las novelas de ciencia ficción y también me encantan las historias de vampiros.

i ....

> Hoy, en el norte del país, hace mucho viento. En el este hace sol por la mañana, pero va a llover por la tarde.

ii ....

> Mi amiga Julia es muy guapa. Es alta y delgada. Tiene el pelo moreno, largo y rizado. Tiene los ojos marrones.

iii ....

> De primer plato, tenemos ensalada de mariscos o gazpacho. De segundo, hay pollo asado o gambas a la plancha. De postre, hay flan, helado o fruta.

iv ....

Films
Food
Hometown and local area
Leisure activities
Personality
Physical description
Weather

b Read the texts again and circle Ⓐ the words that fit in the topic group you selected.

2 **a** Read the texts and circle Ⓐ the correct topic (A or B).

> Este modelo es el más rápido con **una velocidad** máxima de 200 kilómetros por hora. Además, es el más lujoso y más cómodo de la nueva serie. Debajo de los asientos de detrás, hay **un cajón** especial para poner los portátiles, el monedero, los móviles o las cámaras.

i   A   home and contents   B   transport and travel

> Acabamos de salir del estadio. ¡El partido fue fantástico! Vamos a coger un taxi porque está lloviendo y hay muchísima gente haciendo cola para entrar al metro – incluyendo **los hinchas** del otro equipo, ¡todos de mal humor por **la derrota**!

ii   A   sports and leisure activities   B   climate and weather

b Underline Ⓐ the words or phrases that helped you choose the topic of each text.

3 In **2**, you have identified the words that suggest the topic groups. Now see if the words you underlined will help you work out the meaning of the words in bold. Circle Ⓐ the correct answer.

a una velocidad   a price   a size   a speed

b un cajón   a seat   a box   a light

c los hinchas   the supporters   the stadium staff   the groundsmen

d la derrota   the victory   the defeat   the weather

Your turn!

Here is an exam-style question which you can use to practise the skills you have learned, particularly how identifying the topic words belong to can help you understand the text. 🖊

The best apps

You find a list of Spanish apps on a website. Read the descriptions.

A	*En forma*
	Esta aplicación sirve para cualquier actividad al aire libre: correr, andar o caminar. Le indica rutas y distancias recorridas, además del tiempo y las calorías usadas.
B	*Sabelotodo*
	Tiene una base de datos donde puedes buscar las respuestas sobre ciencias o matemáticas.
C	*Organízate*
	La mejor manera de organizar las tareas o los deberes en casa, en el instituto o en la oficina. Se puede guardar qué tareas hay que hacer y las fechas para hacerlas.
D	*Lengua mundo*
	Esta aplicación funciona en el móvil y en el ordenador. Cada lección tiene ejercicios para hablar, escuchar y traducir otros idiomas.
E	*Dónde y cuándo*
	Si buscas información sobre las fechas y los detalles de eventos importantes del pasado, esta aplicación es ideal.
F	*Pásalobien*
	Si haces un viaje largo y quieres entretener a tus hijos pequeños, esta aplicación ofrece un montón de juegos educativos.

Choose the best app for each person. Write the correct letter in each box.

1 My son needs to plan his study time and not be late with homework. ☐ **(1 mark)**

2 It would be useful to measure how far and how fast I run. ☐ **(1 mark)**

3 My aunt wants to learn Chinese but she hasn't got a smartphone. ☐ **(1 mark)**

4 My children ask me questions about Physics homework that I can't answer. ☐ **(1 mark)**

Your turn!

Here is an exam-style question which you can use to practise the skills you have learnt, particularly how spotting synonyms and antonyms can help you to understand the text.

Look for words in the text that mean the same or are the opposite of these words:

fiel   divertido   paciente   optimista   me gusta

Exam-style question

Read this letter about friendship in an online magazine.

Un(a) buen(a) amigo/a tiene que ser leal; eso es lo más importante. Debe ayudarte cuando tienes problemas y apoyarte en todo. Siempre debe decirte la verdad. Tengo un amigo estupendo que se llama Daniel. Me divierto con él porque es muy gracioso y me hace reír. Nos llevamos muy bien y casi nunca discutimos. Lo bueno de nuestra amistad es que somos muy distintos de carácter. Daniel es muy tranquilo y casi siempre está de buen humor, mientras yo suelo ser impaciente, demasiado seria y bastante pesimista. Además, no compartimos las mismas aficiones: a él le encanta descargar y escuchar música rock a todo volumen y a mí no me gusta nada. A mí me chifla leer ciencia ficción y Daniel prefiere las historias de vampiros.

Answer the following questions **in English**.

1   According to the writer, what is the most important quality of a best friend?

.... (1 mark)

2   Why does she have fun when she's with Daniel?

.... (1 mark)

3   According to the writer, what is the advantage of her friendship with Daniel?

.... (1 mark)

4   Who would you say is more optimistic, Daniel or the writer?

.... (1 mark)

5   How does their taste in books differ?

.... (1 mark)

Review your skills

Check up

Review your responses to the exam-style questions on pages 23 and 24. Tick ✓ the column that shows how well you think you have done each of the following.

	Not quite ✓	Nearly there ✓	Got it! ✓
recognised synonyms	☐	☐	☐
recognised antonyms	☐	☐	☐
recognised words that belong to the same topic	☐	☐	☐

Need more practice?

Go back to pages 18 and 19 and complete 🖉 the two exam-style questions there. Use the checklist to help you.

Checklist In my answers, have I ...	✓
read the English introduction to the question in order to understand the context and predict the vocabulary?	
looked for synonyms?	
identified antonyms?	
identified sets of words that belong to the same topic?	

In literary texts as well as in other exam texts there will always be words you don't know. But don't focus on these. Always start by looking for words and phrases you do know. They will help you to get an idea of what the text is about, and in turn, this will help you with the vocabulary you're not familiar with.

How confident do you feel about each of these **skills**? Colour in 🖉 the bars.

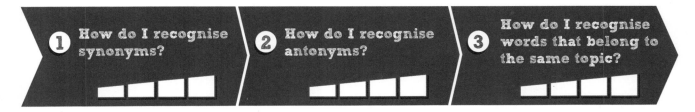

1 How do I recognise synonyms?
2 How do I recognise antonyms?
3 How do I recognise words that belong to the same topic?

Identifying relevant information

This unit will help you learn to identify the information needed to answer the question. The skills you will build are to:

- make sure you understand question words
- locate answers in a text
- deal with unfamiliar words.

In the exam, you will be asked to do reading tasks similar to the ones below. This unit will prepare you to tackle these questions and choose or come up with the best answers.

Do not answer this question yet. You will be asked to come back to it at the end of the unit.

With this style of question, you have to scan the whole text to find the relevant information.

Exam-style question

Hoy en la televisión

Ves la lista de programas de televisión en un periódico. Lee la información.

A	Cocineros de primera Los concursantes compiten para ser el mejor de todos. Esta semana, tienen que aprovechar al máximo los productos de su zona para preparar un plato regional.
B	La vida de los animales Conoceremos los secretos de los desiertos y los grandes espacios abiertos en África y en Sudamérica.
C	Así es el mañana Infórmate sobre los últimos desarrollos en el mundo de la informática. Todo lo que necesitas saber sobre los aparatos más útiles para la vida moderna.
D	Gran Hermano Acaban de entrar en la casa los nuevos habitantes que vivirán juntos durante las próximas semanas. Las cámaras los filmarán 24 horas al día.
E	Diario deportivo Fórmula 1, Gran Premio en el circuito de Cataluña y MotoGP desde Holanda. A ver quiénes toman el liderazgo de los campeonatos.
F	Minimundo Una hora de dibujos animados y programas infantiles. Los niños se divertirán con actividades divertidas y educativas.

¿Cuál es el programa ideal para cada persona? Escribe la letra correcta en cada casilla.

1 Las carreras de coches son muy emocionantes.　　　　　　　　　　　　(1 mark)

2 Quiero ver algo entretenido con mis hijos pequeños.　　　　　　　　　(1 mark)

3 Me encantan los programas informativos sobre la naturaleza.　　　　　(1 mark)

4 Veo todos los programas sobre comida.　　　　　　　　　　　　　　(1 mark)

Get started

Do not answer this question yet. You will be asked to come back to it at the end of the unit.

Exam-style question

Look at the title of the article to find out what it is about. If you don't know what all the words mean, focus on the words you *do* know.

La juventud española y el tiempo libre

Ves este artículo sobre el tiempo libre en una revista.

> ¿Con quién prefieren pasar sus ratos libres los jóvenes españoles? ¿Y qué suelen hacer? La mayoría dice que le gusta estar con los amigos y los pasatiempos mencionados más a menudo son dar una vuelta, ir al cine o ir de excursión. ¿Cómo contactan con sus amigos y compañeros para salir? Pues, con el móvil; esa sí es la respuesta de todos.
>
> ¿Cuáles son sus deportes preferidos? El fútbol, desde luego, sobre todo entre los chicos, pero ahora hay cada vez más equipos femeninos. Se practican también el baloncesto, la natación y el ciclismo.
>
> ¿Dónde pasan la mayoría de sus horas libres los jóvenes? En casa, para estudiar, leer, escuchar música, ver deportes y películas, y para descansar.

Escribe la letra correcta en cada casilla.

1   ¿Qué actividad prefieren los jóvenes?

A	ver una película en casa
B	ir de paseo
C	jugar a los videojuegos

(1 mark)

2   ¿Cómo se ponen en contacto con sus amigos?

A	en el instituto
B	por teléfono
C	en el polideportivo

(1 mark)

3   ¿Cómo es diferente el fútbol hoy día?

A	juegan más chicas
B	el fútbol es menos popular
C	solo es popular entre los chicos

(1 mark)

4   ¿Cuál es otro deporte popular, según el texto?

A	montar en bicicleta
B	montar a caballo
C	montar una tienda

(1 mark)

5   ¿Dónde pasan los jóvenes la mayor parte de su tiempo?

A	al aire libre
B	en la calle
C	dentro de la casa

(1 mark)

The three key questions in the **skills boosts** will help you to improve how you answer this style of question.

 1 How do I make sure I understand question words?

 2 How do I locate answers in a text?

 3 How do I deal with unfamiliar words?

1 How do I make sure I understand question words?

For some exam tasks, you will answer questions in Spanish about a Spanish text, so it is very important to learn all question words well.

(1) Write ✎ the correct English question word beside each Spanish word.

| who | what | where | when | why | which | how | how much |

a qué ....

b quién ....

c cuándo ....

d dónde ....

e cuánto ....

f cómo ....

g cuál ....

h por qué ....

> The question words *quién*, *cuánto* and *cuál* are adjectives in some questions and agree with the noun that they precede. For example: *¿**Quiénes** fueron al cine? ¿**Cuántas** horas al día trabajas? ¿**Cuáles** son tus libros preferidos?*

(2) Read the questions focusing on the question words. What does each one tell you about the information it is asking for? Choose an idea for each one. Write ✎ it beside the question.

| a number | a person | a place | a reason | a time | an activity | a choice |

a ¿Dónde viven tus abuelos? *a place* ....

b ¿Cuáles son los regalos más adecuados para tus padres, un libro y un CD o dos entradas para un concierto? ....

c ¿Quién es tu modelo a seguir? ....

d ¿Por qué admiras a esta persona? ....

e ¿Cuántas veces has visto tu película favorita? ....

f ¿Cuándo estudias mejor, por la mañana o por la tarde? ....

g ¿Qué quieres hacer este fin de semana? ....

(3) a Match ✎ each of the following answers below to the correct question in (2). Use the idea you have written beside each question to help you.

b Circle Ⓐ the word or phrase in the answers that links to each idea you wrote in (2).

i Las entradas, porque les encanta la música.

ii Cinco creo. ¡O quizás más!

iii En Sudamérica, por eso no los veo muy a menudo.

iv Por la tarde, porque por la mañana soy muy dormilón.

v Ir al cine con mis amigos.

vi Mi hermano mayor.

vii Porque es inteligente, trabajadora y simpática.

2 How do I locate answers in a text?

Start by reading the text. Next, read through the questions. Then look at each question in turn and find the answer for each one as you read through the text again.

1 Read about Natalia Tena. Then read the questions. What information does each one ask you to find? Underline Ⓐ the key words in each question and highlight 🖉 the word or words in the text that give you the information. Write 🖉 the letter of the corresponding question (a–f) above the highlighted words.

> **Natalia Tena, actriz y cantante**
>
> *a*
> Natalia Tena es actriz y cantante. Nació en Londres en 1984 y es de nacionalidad británica.
>
> Habla inglés y español porque sus padres son de España. Además, habla vasco, el idioma del
>
> País Vasco, la región del norte de España de donde proviene su padre.
>
> Natalia es la cantante del grupo Molotov Jukebox y también toca el acordeón. Como actriz,
>
> ha salido en las películas de Harry Potter y en la serie de televisión *Juego de tronos*.

a What kind of <u>work</u> does Natalia Tena do?

b Where is she from?

c How many languages does she speak?

d Which part of Spain is her father from?

e Which instrument does Natalia play?

f Which TV series has she appeared in?

2 Write 🖉 the answers to the questions in ① in English on paper.

3 Match 🖉 the statements with the questions. Underline Ⓐ the Spanish and English words that helped you make the link between the questions and the answers.

A Lo que más me gusta es <u>salir con mis amigos</u> a <u>charlar</u> y pasar el rato.	**a** Who is active and sporty?
B Toco el teclado y me encanta todo tipo de música, especialmente la electrónica.	**b** Who prefers <u>socialising</u> as a free time activity?
C Me gusta hacer deporte. Juego al fútbol y al voleibol. ¡Me gusta ganar!	**c** Who relaxes by watching TV?
D No soy teleadicto, pero para descansar, me encanta ver comedias y series policiacas.	**d** Who likes artistic hobbies best?
E Me encanta la lectura y siempre leo un capítulo de mi última novela antes de dormir.	**e** Whose likes to watch his favourite sport?
F Prefiero las actividades creativas y me gusta mucho pintar, sobre todo paisajes.	**f** Who plays an instrument?
G Para mí, lo mejor es seguir mi equipo de rugby e ir al estadio para ver los partidos.	**g** Who enjoys a book at bedtime?

3 How do I deal with unfamiliar words?

You can deal with a word you don't know by looking at its context. Look at the rest of the phrase or the sentence and try to work out the meaning.

1 a Read these extracts from a music festival website. You might not know the words in bold. Highlight ✏ the words you know that can help you work out their meaning. Look at the example to help you.

es ideal para: is ideal for
porque hay música fantástica: because there is great music

> Este festival es ideal para los más **i melómanos** porque hay música fantástica y muy variada. La lista de los grupos de este año están en los **ii carteles** que puedes ver en los sitios públicos y en internet. El festival **iii tiene lugar** del 27 al 29 de abril. La entrada cuesta 65 euros con zona de **iv acampada** incluida para dormir. Pero si no quieres llevar tu propia **v tienda**, la organización te la alquila por pocos euros. Este año **vi encabezan** el reparto *Los Locos y Kaos Urbano* y hay más de 140 grupos en total.

b Now underline Ⓐ the correct option for each word.

i **melómanos** football fans / <u>music lovers</u> / dance fans

ii **carteles** tickets / menus / posters

iii **tiene lugar** takes place / is on sale / is sold out

iv **acampada** cooking / showers / camping

v **tienda** shop / tent / sun hat

vi **encabezan** aren't playing / are supporting / are headlining

- You can also look for cognates and near-cognates. For example, 'acampada' is similar to 'camping'.
- To understand a word like 'encabezan', you can see a Spanish word within it that you know: 'cabeza' meaning 'head'.

2 Read the comments about films, books and TV series. Which word from the list would you expect to find in the gap in each sentence? Then fill in ✏ the gaps with the correct words.

decepcionante(s)	disappointing	escalofriante (s)	frightening, chilling
emocionante (s)	exciting	impresionante(s)	impressive

Example: Prefiero las películas de acción y de aventuras porque son más <u>emocionantes</u> que las comedias y las películas de amor.

a El último episodio de la serie fue bastante .... No era tan bueno como los otros.

b Anoche fuimos al cine y vimos una película de terror. ¡Qué miedo! Era

....

c La última novela de Ruiz Zafón es .... por los personajes que se presentan y por el estilo ágil de la narración.

3 Circle Ⓐ the words in the sentences in **2** that helped you choose the correct missing word and explain ✏ your choice on paper. Look at the example to help you.

Example: *Action and adventure films are likely to be 'exciting'.*

Your turn!

Here is an exam-style question for you to practise the skills you have worked on, specifically how to deal with unfamiliar words. 🖉

Exam-style question

Guide to summer activities

Read an extract from a leaflet about summer activities.

A Gimcana acuática: juegos y concursos dentro y fuera del agua

¿Dónde?	En la playa
¿Cuándo?	De lunes a viernes, de las 10.30 a las 12.00
¿Para quién?	Niños a partir de los 4 años (imprescindible saber nadar)
¿Cuánto?	Gratuita

B Visita al museo romano

¿Dónde?	San Martí d'Empuries
¿Cuándo?	De las 10.00 a las 18.00 (cerrado los lunes)
¿Cuánto?	5 euros (3 euros mayores de 65 años; menores de 8 años entrada gratuita)

Use the context to work out the meaning of 'imprescindible'. Also, use logic and your powers of deduction: it's a water activity, so being able to swim is essential.

Answer the following questions **in English**.

Example: Where do the games and competitions take place? <u>on the beach and in the water</u>

1 On what days are the games and competitions held? .... **(1 mark)**

2 Who are these activities intended for? .... **(1 mark)**

3 What must participants be able to do? .... **(1 mark)**

4 When is the Roman museum closed? .... **(1 mark)**

5 Who can get in to the museum for free? .... **(1 mark)**

Your turn!

Here is an exam-style question for you to practise the skills you have worked on, specifically how to locate information in a text. 🖉

Exam-style question

Young people and sport

You read this article in a Spanish magazine about the benefits of sport.

> **¿Qué tiene que ver el deporte con la salud?**
>
> Los jóvenes que practican deporte tendrán menos problemas de salud en su futuro adulto.
>
> **¿Cuánto tiempo deben dedicar los jóvenes al deporte?**
>
> Se recomienda entre 30 minutos y una hora al día.
>
> **¿Cuáles son las ventajas del deporte?**
>
> Se recomienda practicar deportes desde la niñez para evitar problemas como la obesidad y la depresión. Además, las actividades deportivas ayudan a los adolescentes a ser más disciplinados.

Notice how the question words in the text match the questions in the task. They will help you find the answers.

Look for cognates and near-cognates in the text to help you understand unfamiliar words. Look at Unit 2, pages 10–13 for more information.

Answer the following questions **in English**.

1   What is the long-term benefit of doing sport from a young age?

    ....   (1 mark)

2   How much exercise should a young person do on a daily basis?

    ....   (1 mark)

3   Which benefits of doing sport from childhood are mentioned?

    Give **two** details.

    ....

    ....   (2 marks)

Review your skills

Check up

Review your responses to the exam-style questions on pages 31 and 32. Tick ✓ the column that shows how well you think you have done each of the following.

	Not quite ✓	Nearly there ✓	Got it! ✓
understood question words	☐	☐	☐
located answers in a text	☐	☐	☐
dealt with unfamiliar words	☐	☐	☐

Need more practice?

Go back to pages 26 and 27 and complete ✎ the two exam-style questions there. Use the checklist to help you.

Checklist Before I give my answers, have I ...	✓
read each text to get the gist of what it is about?	
then looked carefully for the answer to each question?	
understood the question words where relevant?	
used the context to help me understand unfamiliar words?	
used logic, deduction, and other clues to help me understand unfamiliar words?	
used other related Spanish words I know to help me understand unfamiliar words?	

You should never rush to tick or fill in an answer. Always check twice even if the answer seems obvious at first: some options can be confusing and are meant to make you read the text very closely!

How confident do you feel about each of these **skills**? Colour in ✎ the bars.

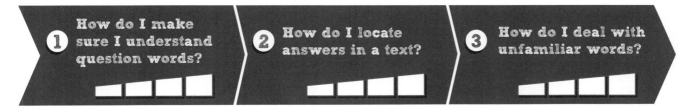

1. How do I make sure I understand question words?

2. How do I locate answers in a text?

3. How do I deal with unfamiliar words?

⑤ Using grammatical clues

This unit will help you use grammar to understand a text. The skills you will build are to:

- make use of time phrases to help your understanding
- make use of tenses to clarify meaning
- make use of verb endings to clarify meaning.

In the exam, you will be asked to tackle reading tasks such as the ones on these two pages. This unit will prepare you to write your response to these questions.

Do not answer this question yet. You will be asked to come back to it at the end of the unit.

Exam-style question

Read the text about Felipe, a poor student, who is out with his boss, Alejandro.

> **_El doctor Centeno_ by Benito Pérez Galdós**
>
> Eran las nueve y cuarto.
>
> Aunque era domingo, muchas tiendas estaban abiertas. Pasaron por una zapatería, cuyo iluminado escaparate contenía variedad de calzado* para ambos sexos.
>
> 'Para, cochero*' gritó Alejandro. 'Y tú, Felipe, baja. Te voy a comprar unas botas.'
>
> Felipe bajó gozoso; entró en la tienda. Al poco rato volvió a decir a su amo*:
>
> 'Me he puesto unas… Pide cincuenta y seis reales*.'
>
> 'Toma el dinero, paga y ven al momento.'
>
> Al poco rato volvió a aparecer el gran Felipe llevando las botas nuevas y con las viejas en la mano.
>
> '¿Qué hago con éstas?'
>
> 'Tira eso, tíralas…'
>
> Felipe las tiró en medio de la calle, no sin cierto desconsuelo porque las botas, aunque feas, todavía servían, (…) y no le gustaba tirar cosa alguna.
>
> * calzado = footwear   * amo = boss
> * cochero = driver   * reales = old Spanish coin

Answer the following questions **in English**.

1   What day of the week was it when Felipe and Alejandro went shopping?

   .... (1 mark)

2   Who was going to pay for Felipe's new boots?

   .... (1 mark)

3   Where did Alejandro throw his old boots?

   .... (1 mark)

4   Why was Felipe not happy to do what Alejandro asked him?

   .... (1 mark)

To help you understand a text in Spanish you need to recognise when the action is taking place by correctly identifying tenses and time phrases. As well as knowing **when** an event is happening, it is also important to focus on the verb endings to see **who** is doing the action.

(1) Read the text below. There are verbs in the past, the present and the future. Underline (A) all the verbs and write (✐) on paper the time frame each one represents.

Do not answer this question yet. You will be asked to come back to it at the end of the unit.

Exam-style question

A village in summer

Your Spanish friend, Marina, sends you this email.

> Este verano estoy en el pueblo de mis abuelos, en el campo y lejos de la ciudad. Es un sitio muy tranquilo y no hay mucho que hacer para los jóvenes. Lo mejor del pueblo es que tiene una piscina al aire libre y mañana voy a pasar el día allí con mis primos; será muy divertido. También, cada año celebran una fiesta muy alegre en el pueblo. No fui el año pasado porque estuve en la costa con mis padres, pero este año voy a ir. Empieza el próximo sábado con un espectáculo de fuegos artificiales.

When does each event take place?

Write **P** for something that happened in the **past**.

Write **N** for something that is happening **now**.

Write **F** for something that is going to happen in the **future**.

Write the correct letter in each box.

1	spending summer in her grandparent's village	(1 mark)
2	going to the swimming pool	(1 mark)
3	going to the coast with her parents	(1 mark)
4	going to the village festival	(1 mark)

> To help you, make sure you look for clues in the time phrases as well as in the tenses of the verbs.

The three key questions in the **skills boosts** will help you to use grammar to understand a text.

 1 How do I make use of time phrases to help my understanding?

 2 How do I make use of tenses to clarify meaning?

 3 How do I make use of verb endings to clarify meaning?

1 How do I make use of time phrases to help my understanding?

To help you work out when an event is taking place, look carefully in the text to find phrases that refer to times and dates. These can be single words like *ahora* (now), *ayer* (yesterday) or *mañana* (tomorrow) or short phrases like *hace dos años* (two years ago), *el martes que viene* (next Tuesday) or *esta noche* (tonight).

① Look at the words and phrases in the box. Write 🖉 the correct letter next to each one: P for Past, N for Now and F for Future.

pasado mañana		anoche		esta noche		ahora	
anteayer		el julio pasado		mañana por la tarde		ayer	
de momento		hace dos semanas		el lunes que viene		hoy	
el mes próximo		en el porvenir		a partir de mañana		hace un siglo	

Make a list of useful time phrases and learn them.

② **a** These people are talking about their towns. Read the sentences and highlight 🖉 the time words and phrases.

  i   Todos los sábados voy al centro de la ciudad con mis amigos.

  ii Mi pueblo es bastante tranquilo, pero hace muchos años era muy industrial.

  iii De momento, estoy en el café, tomando un zumo de naranja.

  iv La semana próxima, hay una gran feria en la ciudad.

  v   Ahora no hay muchos habitantes, pero antes era un pueblo animado.

  vi El mercado es muy barato y, a partir del sábado que viene, voy a hacer la compra allí.

  vii Nos gustó mucho el festival de cine que se celebró el mes pasado.

  b Read the sentences in **a** again. Then read the events in English below. When does each event take place? Write 🖉 P for Past, N for Now and F for Future in each box. Use the time phrases you highlighted in **a** to help you.

  Notice that the events are not in the same order as the sentences in 2a.

  i   Drinking orange juice in a café   ☐

  ii A big fair coming to town   ☐

  iii Film festival taking place   ☐

  iv Shopping in the market   ☐

  v   The town being very industrial   ☐

2 How do I make use of tenses to clarify meaning?

The texts you have to read often combine verbs in the present, past and future tenses.
- Recognise their forms by learning common verb patterns.
- Understand which of the verb patterns relate to which time frame.

1 Look at the literary extract *El Libro de los cuentos*.

> *El libro de los cuentos* by Rafael Boira
>
> **Las tiendas abiertas**
>
> Una amiga nuestra solía decir:
>
> — Están tan frías las tiendas que tienes que llevar un abrigo para ir de compras. La última vez que fui cogí un constipado, pero no puedo resistir entrar en ellas porque están siempre abiertas.
>
> — Pues buen remedio, un amigo le contestó. 'Debes ir solo los días de fiesta por la tarde y las encontrarás cerradas.'

a First, underline (A) all the verbs you can find.

b Then identify and annotate the tense of each of the verbs.

2 a Read events (i–iv) below and highlight the section of the text in **1** that contains the answer to each event.

b Read the text in **1** again and the events below. When does each event take place?

Write **P** for something that happened in the **past**.

Write **N** for something that is happening **now**.

Write **F** for something that is going to happen in the **future**.

Write the correct letter in each box.

i friend commenting about cold shops (1 mark)

ii catching a cold (1 mark)

iii not being able to resist going into shops (1 mark)

iv finding shops closed (1 mark)

Check you know the verb endings.

Past: could be the Imperfect: **-aba** endings for **-ar** verbs and **-ía** endings for **-ir** and **-er** verbs or the Preterite: (**-ar** verbs) -é, -aste, -ó, -amos, -asteis, -aron (**-er** and **-ir** verbs) -í, -iste, -ió, -imos, -isteis, -ieron

Future: -é, -ás, -á, emos, --éis, -án OR voy, vas, va, vamos, vais, van a + infinitive

3 How do I make use of verb endings to clarify meaning?

In order to identify the subject of the verb (i.e. who or what is doing the action of the verb), it is essential to look at the verb ending.

> Remember that subject pronouns are not always used in Spanish, but ensure you pay attention to them when they are used: *yo, tú, él/ella/usted, nosotros/as, vosotros/as, ellos/ellas/ustedes.*

1 a José talks about a shopping trip. Underline Ⓐ all the verbs in the text.

> Quise comprar unas botas nuevas para el invierno. La zapatería estaba en la calle principal, pero no la encontraba. Pedí direcciones a un hombre y me contestó; 'No está abierta de momento; mejor ir a los grandes almacenes.' Tomé un autobús que me llevó allí. Una dependienta me preguntó qué quería. Le contesté que quería unas botas. 'No tenemos muchas en verano,' ella me respondió. '¿Ves dónde están las sandalias? Pues, las botas se encuentran a la derecha.'

b Now write 🖉 the verbs and note down 🖉 who or what is doing each action, choosing one of the possible answers from the box.

> Notice that José is telling the story, so all verbs with the 1st person singular ending (such as *quise* – I wanted) will be referring to José.

| boots | bus | José | man | sandals | shoe shop | shop assistant | we |

....

....

....

....

....

2 Who is doing the action of the verbs that are underlined in these sentences? Circle Ⓐ the correct subject.

> Do not be misled by words in front of the verb.
> Example: *Pilar me regaló un collar.* (*regaló* means 'she gave')
> Meaning: Pilar gave a necklace <u>to me</u> as a present. (not 'I' gave the present to 'her').

a Ana y yo fuimos al restaurante con mi padre y nos <u>compró</u> una pizza.   *Ana and I / Ana's father*

b Pedro, tu mamá te <u>dará</u> la lista para hacer la compra.   *Pedro / Pedro's mother*

c Estos planos de la ciudad me <u>muestran</u> los sitios de interés.   *I / the street plans*

d Perdí a mi amiga en el centro, pero la <u>encontré</u> en el mercado.   *I / my friend*

e Cogimos el autobús que nos <u>llevó</u> directamente al cine.   *We / the bus*

Your turn!

Here is an exam-style question which requires you to put into practice the skills you have worked on, specifically how to apply your knowledge of time phrases, tenses and verb endings. 🖉

Ensure you use your knowledge of time phrases, tenses and verb endings to answer these questions accurately.

Exam-style question

Your Spanish friend, Roberto, has written an article about his town for the school magazine.

> Mi pueblo ya no es lo que era y, hoy en día, muchos critican el aumento en el número de hoteles grandes, apartamentos y restaurantes de comida rápida. Mi abuelo recuerda cómo era en su juventud cuando la agricultura era la industria principal y había tan poco tráfico que los perros dormían en medio de la calle. La gente que trabajaba en los campos ahora tiene empleos en el turismo y los jóvenes copian la moda y los gustos de los extranjeros. Tengo la impresión de que, dentro de diez años, mi pueblo ya no será como un pueblo español porque estará lleno de bares irlandeses, cafés que ofrecen 'desayuno inglés' y hamburgueserías americanas.

Which period does each phrase describe?

Write **P** for a description of the **past**.

Write **N** for a description of **now**.

Write **F** for a description of the **future**.

Write the correct letter in each box.

1   people criticising the town's development   ☐   (1 mark)

2   agriculture being the main industry   ☐   (1 mark)

3   young people imitating the tourists   ☐   (1 mark)

4   the town losing its identity   ☐   (1 mark)

Your turn!

This is another exam-style question which requires you to put into practice the skills you have worked on, specifically analysing sentences for grammatical clues. 🖉

Exam-style question

You read this story about Marcos and the Rastro market in Madrid.

> Para Marcos, el mejor lugar para pasar la mañana los domingos en Madrid era el mercado del Rastro. Iba a hacer fotos, tomarse un café o encontrarse con amigos.
>
> Esta mañana va de camino al Rastro en busca de artículos antiguos y cosas raras. Viaja en metro porque es imposible aparcar. Quiere llegar para las diez; más tarde habrá demasiada gente.
>
> El Mercado se extiende a lo largo de varias calles y en ellas hay puestos con ropa, zapatos, alimentos, artesanía, antigüedades… Una vez Marcos compró unos pendientes muy bonitos y se los regaló a una amiga. Más tarde descubrieron que eran muy antiguos y valiosos. Marcos vuelve al mercado cada domingo, diciéndose que un día encontrará más tesoros.

When does each event take place?

Write **P** for something that happened in the **past**.

Write **N** for something that is happening **now**.

Write **F** for something that is going to happen in the **future**.

Write the correct letter in each box.

1 taking photos ☐ (1 mark)

2 looking for antiques ☐ (1 mark)

3 travelling on the underground ☐ (1 mark)

4 buying earrings ☐ (1 mark)

5 finding treasure ☐ (1 mark)

Analyse the sentences you are not sure about and identify the verb(s) and the subject(s). What tense is the main verb in?

Review your skills

Check up

Review your responses to the exam-style questions on pages 39 and 40. Tick ✓ the column that shows how well you think you have done each of the following.

	Not quite ✓	Nearly there ✓	Got it! ✓
made use of time phrases to help my understanding	☐	☐	☐
made use of tenses to clarify meaning	☐	☐	☐
made use of verb endings to clarify meaning	☐	☐	☐

Need more practice?

Go back to pages 34 and 35 and complete 🖊 the two exam-style questions there. Use the checklist to help you.

Checklist In my answers have I...	✓
read the introduction to the question in order to understand the context and predict the vocabulary?	
read through the text *and* the questions?	
identified any time words or phrases to help my understanding?	
analysed the sentences, looking for verb and subject to help my understanding?	
identified the tenses in the sentences?	

Remember that in an exam situation, you're looking to answer the questions. Don't worry about the parts of the text that are not relevant to those questions!

How confident do you feel about each of these **skills**? Colour in 🖊 the bars.

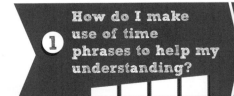

1. How do I make use of time phrases to help my understanding?

2. How do I make use of tenses to clarify meaning?

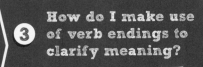

3. How do I make use of verb endings to clarify meaning?

⑥ Giving clear answers with appropriate detail

This unit will help you to learn how to give clear answers with just the right amount of detail required. The skills that you will build are to:

- avoid ambiguous or contradictory answers
- make sure your answers are sufficiently detailed
- avoid including irrelevant information.

In the exam, you will be asked to do reading tasks similar to these. This unit will prepare you to tackle these questions and write the best answers in English.

Do not answer this question yet. You will be asked to come back to it at the end of the unit.

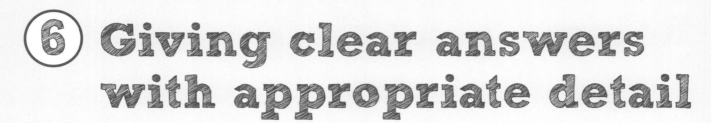

Exam-style question

Eating out

You are researching restaurants online and find this advert.

> En el barrio madrileño de Chamberí, cerca de la estación de tren, se encuentra un espectacular restaurante que te recibe con trato amistoso y agradable hasta en el nombre: *Flor de Amor*.
>
> Tienes que visitar este lugar si buscas un estilo completamente diferente y moderno donde puedes gozar de recetas sencillas de la cocina tradicional francesa.
>
> Ofrecemos un 40% de descuento si consumes como mínimo un primero y un segundo. Disfruta de nuestra promoción de lunes a viernes en comidas y los sábados y domingos en cenas. *Flor de Amor* es una gran elección para todas las ocasiones, visítalo.

Answer the following questions **in English**.

1 Where is the restaurant close to?

.... (1 mark)

2 What sort of welcome will you receive?

.... (1 mark)

3 What sort of food does the restaurant serve?

.... (1 mark)

4 How many courses do you need to order to get a discount?

.... (1 mark)

5 What meal is on special offer on weekdays?

.... (1 mark)

In exam tasks there are different styles of questions: some require you to pick the exact information from the text, others ask you to make deductions. It is important to learn to identify the question types as it can help you to select the appropriate information from the text.

① Look at the three questions in the exam-style task below. What style of questions are they? Tick ✓ the correct answer.

deduction ☐   fact ☐

Do not answer this question yet. You will be asked to come back to it at the end of the unit.

Exam-style question

Celebrations and festivals

You read this article on a Spanish website.

> Cumpleaños, aniversarios, fiestas de navidad… Si nos paramos a pensar por un momento en todas las fiestas en las que podríamos derrochar dinero, nos entraría un ataque de nervios. Normalmente creemos que gastar mucho dinero es necesario para demostrar el aprecio hacia una persona.
>
> Sin embargo, un regalo no tiene por qué ser caro y dará el mismo placer o más que otro con un precio alto. El día de mi cumpleaños mi hermano menor se pasó una tarde entera haciéndome una tarjeta preciosa. Este detalle tan personal me encantó. ¡Me gustó más que todos los demás regalos que recibí!

Answer the following questions **in English**.

1   What did the writer's brother do for her birthday?

.... (1 mark)

2   What did the writer think of her brother's gesture?

.... (1 mark)

3   How does the writer feel about presents and their cost?

.... (1 mark)

The three key questions in the **skills boosts** will help you to improve how you answer these types of questions.

 How do I avoid wrong, ambiguous and contradictory answers?

 How do I make sure my answers are sufficiently detailed?

 How do I avoid including irrelevant information?

1 How do I avoid wrong, ambiguous and contradictory answers?

You need to make sure the answers you give make sense. First, make sure you know what the questions are asking. Then select the exact bit of information in the text, make sure you understand it and choose the correct option.

(1) Read the following descriptions of special occasions and look at the sample answers given by three different students. Tick ⊘ the correct answer. Put a cross ⊗ against the wrong answers and explain ⟨✐⟩ why they are wrong.

> **Carmela:** Anoche cenamos en un restaurante italiano que está muy cerca de mi casa. Prefiero la comida china, pero fuimos para celebrar el cumpleaños de mi abuela. Nos gustaron mucho los postres.

Example: Why did Carmela go to the restaurant with her family?

She likes Italian (italiano) food. ✗ *Contradicts the text; she prefers Chinese food.*

It's close (cerca) to home. ✗ *Information not relevant; the restaurant just happens to be close.*

Because it was her grandmother's birthday (cumpleaños) ✓ *good answer*

She likes to eat desserts (postres). ✗ *The question asks 'why' and this is not a reason. The family enjoyed the desserts, but that's a result ....*

> **Xiomara:** Normalmente mis padres y yo celebramos la Nochevieja en casa, aunque a veces voy a una fiesta con amigos. Sin embargo, este año vamos a Colombia, donde se reunirá toda la familia para una gran cena.

a How is Xiomara planning to spend New Year's Eve?

She always stays at home with her parents. ☐ ....

She goes to a party. ☐ ....

She's planning to be in Colombia. ☐ ....

She's celebrating with a family dinner. ☐ ....

> **Carlitos:** Me gusta preparar la comida. Cocino de todo: pescado, sopas, pasteles. Lo que más me gusta hacer es tortilla de patatas, aunque no me gustan mucho los huevos.

b What does Carlitos like to cook the most?

At lunch time ☐ ....

Fish, soup and cakes ☐ ....

Spanish omelette ☐ ....

Chips ☐ ....

2 **How do I make sure my answers are sufficiently detailed?**

Your answers must give the exact information needed to answer the questions, so you must ensure that you have included all relevant details from the text.

1 Read the question after each section of the text about Sofía's visit to a festival. Check you understand the wrong answer that is given and the examiner's comment. Then write ✏ down the correct answer.

> Este marzo fui a Valencia para ver la famosa fiesta de Las Fallas. Quería estar los <u>veinte días</u> que dura la fiesta, pero sólo me quedé <u>una semana</u> porque tenía que trabajar.

The question is asking 'how long' Sofía wanted to stay so look for words to do with time in the text.

Example: <u>How long</u> did Sofía want to stay in Valencia?

~~20~~ insufficient detail, 20 hours, days, weeks or months?

<u>20 days</u>

> Me encantaron los concursos de paella. Probé muchos platos y algunos estaban riquísimos; otros no tanto <u>porque es difícil hacer una paella en la calle para tanta gente.</u>

The question word is asking for reasons, so look for the number of reasons given in the text.

a Why weren't all the paella dishes tasty? Give two details.

Difficult to make a paella. insufficient detail

_____

> Durante el día había desfiles y danzas tradicionales muy bonitos. Por la noche hacían castillos de fuegos artificiales en la plaza que para mí eran aún más espectaculares.

b Why did she prefer the evening activities?

During the day they had parades and dances that were nice. At night they made firework castles in the square which were even more spectacular Too much detail; answer is buried.

_____

> Todas las noches había música y el sábado bailamos hasta la madrugada. Sin embargo, lo mejor para mí fue la última noche cuando quemaron figuras enormes de escenas cómicas y de personas famosas.

c What did the figures depict?

Comic scenes Only half the answer, insufficient detail, therefore incomplete.

_____

③ How do I avoid including irrelevant information?

When answering a question, you must avoid writing too little and not giving enough detail, but equally you must avoid writing too much and risk being penalised for an ambiguous, incomplete or unclear answer. Also, make sure you are not answering a different question from the one set!

① Read this article about a film festival and find the five sections of the text with the answer to each question. Write 🖊 the letter of the question in the box after that section.

La Fiesta del Cine se celebra a partir de este lunes 8 de mayo hasta el miércoles día 10 ☐ en salas de toda España ☐ _a_ ☐, con entradas a solo 2,90 euros ☐. Para conseguir precios reducidos ☐ se debe registrar en la página web www.fiestadelcine.com ☐. Las entradas están ya a la venta ☐ en las taquillas de los cines participantes ☐ y por internet ☐. Se estima que 2,6 millones de personas ☐ asistirán al festival, medio millón más que el año pasado ☐, a pesar de que competirá con la celebración de los partidos de semifinales ☐ de la Liga de Campeones de fútbol los últimos dos días ☐.

a Where is the festival taking place?

b What can you get if you register on-line?

c Give **two** places where you can buy tickets.

d How many more people will go this year compared to last year?

e What else is happening at the same time as the festival?

② Read Andrés' message about a festival. Look at the answers to the questions and cross out ~~cat~~ the information that is not relevant. Explain 🖊 why it is not relevant.

En agosto voy al Festival Internacional de Deportes Extremos en Galicia. Dura tres días y es la competición más grande de deportes extremos en España. Vienen participantes de todas partes del mundo a demostrar sus habilidades. También hay talleres donde puedes aprender algunas de las técnicas deportivas de la mano de los profesionales. Voy porque el festival no solo es deportivo, sino también cultural. Ofrece una gran variedad de espectáculos artísticos, bandas en vivo y DJs.

Example: What type of festival is Andrés going to?

He's going to an extreme sports festival ~~in Galicia~~.
The question doesn't ask about where the festival takes place

a How big is the festival?

It's the biggest in Spain and lasts three days. ....

b Where do the contestants come from?

They come from all over the world to demonstrate their skills. ....

c What can you learn in the workshops?

sports skills at the hands of the experts ....

③ Now go back to ① and answer 🖊 the questions on paper. Remember to look at the question words to help you identify the relevant information.

Your turn!

Here is an exam-style question which requires you to put into practice the skills you have worked on, specifically how to make your answers as clear and appropriately detailed as possible. Too little or too much information could cost you marks! ✏️

Exam-style question

Christmas Eve

You read this blog by Danuta about Christmas Eve in Spain and Poland.

Soy polaca, pero vivo en España y en los dos países el día más importante de Navidad es el 24 de diciembre cuando se reúne toda la familia. En Polonia lo primero que hacemos es buscar la primera estrella en el cielo y después ya la fiesta empieza en serio. Compartimos un pan especial y lo bonito es que damos el pan sagrado a los animales de la casa ya que, según la tradición, en esa noche, los animales hablan el lenguaje humano. Esto no se hace en España.

Luego la familia se sienta a la mesa a compartir la cena navideña igual que nuestros vecinos españoles. Sin embargo, los polacos dejamos una silla libre y un plato vacío por si alguien llama a la puerta.

A medianoche vamos a la iglesia como se hace en España. Lo que echo de menos es que en Polonia, después de la misa, hay grupos de jóvenes, disfrazados de animales que van de casa en casa para cantar villancicos y a cambio de eso hay que darles dulces o dinero.

Don't forget to look at the question words 'who', 'what', 'why', 'when' and 'where' in the question to help you locate your answer in the text.

Answer the following questions **in English**.

1 Who gets together on Christmas Eve in Spain and Poland?

.... (1 mark)

2 What don't Spanish families look for on Christmas Eve?

.... (1 mark)

3 What do Polish people believe animals can do on Christmas Eve?

.... (1 mark)

4 What do both Polish and Spanish families do at midnight on Christmas Eve?

.... (1 mark)

Make sure nothing is missing from your answer, especially if you are asked for two details.

5 Name **two** things carol singers are given in Poland.

.... (2 marks)

Your turn!

Here is an exam-style question which requires you to put into practice the skills you have worked on, specifically how to ensure that your answers are sufficiently detailed without including irrelevant information. ✏️

Exam-style question

Eating cheaply

You read Diego's blog post on a Spanish website.

> Si quieres ahorrar el dinero que gastas en alimentación, es posible comer bien en casa por menos de dos euros al día. Creo que tiramos mucho dinero y muchísima comida. Nos obsesionan las marcas y tenemos miedo de los productos baratos. En mi pueblo es más fácil encontrar un mango de la India que fruta fresca de la zona. Pero, sobre todo, creo que estamos obsesionados por la proteína animal. Comer tanta carne no es sostenible en términos ambientales y desde luego tampoco en términos de salud. Y desde el punto de vista económico, es un sobrecoste innecesario. Creo que sería mucho mejor reducir el consumo de carne y comer más legumbres.

Answer the following questions **in English**.

1 Where does Diego find it hard to find fresh fruit?

   .... (1 mark)

2 What does he say is unsustainable?

   .... (1 mark)

3 What does Diego recommend as a healthier and cheaper way forward?

   .... (1 mark)

Remember that even if a word in the question appears in the text, that does not mean it is definitely the answer.

Read the text closely so you do not miss a negation, for instance, which changes the meaning of a sentence.

Review your skills

Check up

Review your responses to the exam-style questions on pages 47 and 48. Tick ⊘ the column that shows how well you think you have done each of the following.

	Not quite ⊘	Nearly there ⊘	Got it! ⊘
avoided wrong, ambiguous and contradictory answers	☐	☐	☐
made sure my answers are sufficiently detailed	☐	☐	☐
avoided including irrelevant information	☐	☐	☐

Need more practice?

Go back to pages 42 and 43 and complete ⊘ the two exam-style questions there. Use the checklist to help you.

Checklist In my answers have I...	⊘
made sure I have located the answer in the relevant part of the text?	
checked I haven't used words that are in the text, but don't address the question?	
given enough details to make sure the question is answered fully?	
been careful to avoid giving too much information in case it is irrelevant?	

> Remember to read the instructions carefully. When giving your answer, do not write full sentences if you don't need to. Make sure you answer the question with the required amount of detail and do not include irrelevant material.

How confident do you feel about each of these **skills**? Colour in ⊘ the bars.

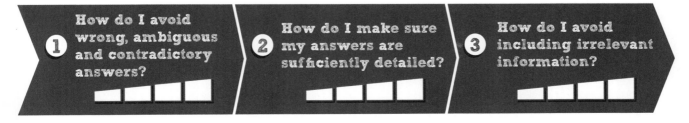

1. How do I avoid wrong, ambiguous and contradictory answers?
2. How do I make sure my answers are sufficiently detailed?
3. How do I avoid including irrelevant information?

7 Using deduction

This unit will help you use your powers of deduction to understand what's not completely explicit in a text. The skills you will build are to:

- recognise positive and negative ideas
- identify opinions and justifications
- answer questions by combining information from different parts of a text.

In the exam, you will be asked to do reading tasks similar to the ones on these two pages. This unit will prepare you to tackle these questions and use inference to come up with the correct answers.

'Inference' means coming to a conclusion, based on the information you have. You need to use inference to understand meaning that is implied (when an idea or opinion is suggested but not stated directly).

Do not answer this question yet. You will be asked to come back to it at the end of the unit.

Exam-style question

Ofertas de empleo

Ves estos anuncios en el periódico.

A	Buscamos personal para trabajar en la recepción de un hotel. Debes tener buen nivel de dos (o más) idiomas.
B	Tienda de ropa y equipo deportivo busca jóvenes para trabajar en verano. Necesitas buena presencia y aptitudes de comunicación para relacionarte con los clientes.
C	Campamento de verano busca monitores para este verano. Vivirás en el campamento y animarás a los niños a participar en actividades deportivas y creativas.
D	Buscamos a dos jóvenes para realizar tareas administrativas durante el verano. Se requiere conocimientos de los programas más comunes que usan los ordenadores.
E	Gran hotel de lujo busca personal de cocina. Experiencia en el mundo de la restauración será una ventaja.
F	*Estadio Sporting* busca a jóvenes para trabajar en la taquilla los días en que hay partidos. Tendrás contacto con el público y trabajarás en la caja.
G	Residencia de ancianos busca personal para ayudar a los residentes con el ejercicio y actividades sociales.

¿Cuál es el mejor trabajo para cada persona? Escribe la letra correcta en cada casilla.

1   Me encanta la informática y la idea de trabajar en una oficina.   ☐   **(1 mark)**

2   Soy activa y deportista. En el futuro voy a ser o profesora o maestra.   ☐   **(1 mark)**

3   Quiero trabajar en turismo. Domino el inglés y el francés.   ☐   **(1 mark)**

4   Me llevo bien con la gente y me gustaría ser dependienta.   ☐   **(1 mark)**

5   Me interesa la comida y me encanta preparar platos regionales.   ☐   **(1 mark)**

Do not answer this question yet. You will be asked to come back to it at the end of the unit.

Exam-style question

Spanish young people working abroad

You see this article on a website for Spanish students.

> El porcentaje de menores de 25 años desempleados es alrededor del 42%. No es de sorprender entonces que el año pasado, casi 100.000 jóvenes buscaron empleo fuera de España, en Europa, Estados Unidos y Australia.
>
> Oriana Torres, 19 años y de Sevilla, nos contó que encontró un puesto de trabajo en una cafetería en Londres. 'Trabajo muchas horas y las tareas son repetitivas: preparo y sirvo café y té desde las 7 de la mañana hasta las 5 de la tarde. Lo bueno es que no tengo tiempo para aburrirme. Me llevo bien con mis compañeros de trabajo: son todos muy simpáticos. A veces hay clientes impacientes, lo que es un poco estresante, pero por lo general, la gente es muy amable. Una ventaja de trabajar aquí es que tengo que hablar inglés todo el día. Al principio no entendía nada, pero ahora hablo bastante bien.'

Write the correct letter in each box.

1 Why do many young people go to other countries?

A	to study
B	to work
C	to learn English

(1 mark)

2 Where does Oriana Torres work?

A	Spain
B	England
C	Australia

(1 mark)

3 What work does Oriana do?

A	waitress
B	receptionist
C	cook

(1 mark)

4 What is the negative aspect of the job?

A	She doesn't earn much money.
B	She doesn't like her colleagues.
C	She does the same every day.

(1 mark)

5 In general, what are the customers like?

A	pleasant
B	rude
C	impatient

(1 mark)

6 What benefit of the job does she mention?

A	She gets to meet a lot of people.
B	She likes the café.
C	Her English has improved.

(1 mark)

The three key questions in the **skills boosts** will help you to improve how you answer these types of questions.

1 How do I recognise positive and negative ideas?

2 How do I identify opinions and justification?

3 How do I answer questions by combining information from different parts of a text?

How do I recognise positive and negative ideas?

For some exam tasks, you will need to show that you can identify and understand positive and negative ideas. To prepare for this, learn key words and phrases from each topic. Also, focus on words and phrases that express positive or negative ideas.

1 Read the adjectives you might use to describe work. Write P for positive or N for negative beside each one.

a variado ☐   **e** repetitivo ☐   **i** aburrido ☐

b duro ☐   **f** útil ☐   **j** divertido ☐

c fácil ☐   **g** difícil ☐   **k** emocionante ☐

d interesante ☐   **h** creativo ☐   **l** monótono ☐

2 Match the Spanish verbs to the English verbs. Then tick ✓ the Spanish verbs that you might use to express a positive idea about work and put a cross ✗ beside any that express a negative idea.

☐	A aprender		**a** to be bored
☐	B aburrirse		**b** to earn (money)
☐	C ayudar		**c** to help
☐	D ganar (dinero)		**d** to improve
☐	E mejorar		**e** to learn
☐	F viajar		**f** to travel

(A aprender is linked to e to learn)

3 Read the sentences. Underline ⒜ the positive ideas and circle Ⓐ the negative ideas.

a El <u>sueldo</u> es muy <u>alto</u> pero tienes que (trabajar muchas horas).

b El horario es flexible y lo bueno es que tienes los fines de semana libres.

c El jefe es bastante severo, pero nos explica bien las tareas.

d El trabajo no era difícil, pero llegó a ser monótono.

e Lo mejor de las prácticas fue que aprendí mucho. Fue una experiencia útil.

f Gané muy poco dinero, pero mejoré mi nivel de español.

g El trabajo no era interesante. Fue una pérdida de tiempo.

> Look out for words and phrases that introduce a positive or negative idea.
>
> **Positive:** lo bueno, lo mejor, la ventaja, afortunadamente, ¡menos mal!
>
> **Negative:** lo malo, lo peor, la desventaja, desafortunadamente

2 How do I recognise opinions and justifications?

The texts you have to read often combine opinions with justifications, i.e. reasons or examples. If you are not sure you have understood the writer's opinion, look for reasons or examples that can give you clues.

To identify opinions in a text, look out for verbs that are connected with ideas (e.g. *pensar*, *creer*, *decir*).

1 Underline (A) the word or phrase in each sentence which introduces an opinion.

a "Creo que es importante aprender idiomas." **Noemí**

b "Nuestros profesores piensan que vale la pena hacer prácticas laborables." **David**

c "En mi opinión, no es necesario pasar la aspiradora todos los días." **Julia**

d "Mi abuelo dice que no importa qué haces, sino cómo lo haces." **Raúl**

e "Para mí, lo más importante es hacer un trabajo útil." **Luisa**

Also, look for words and phrases that imply opinions and learn them in pairs of antonyms, for example: *¡qué bien!* (that's great!) – *¡qué pena!* (what a pity); *estoy de acuerdo* (I agree) – *no estoy de acuerdo* (I disagree).

2 Underline (A) the correct option to match the sense of the rest of the sentence. Highlight (✐) the words that helped you work out the correct answer.

a Si quieres trabajar en el extranjero, es *una ventaja / una desventaja* no hablar otros idiomas.

b Hacer prácticas laborables *vale la pena / es una pérdida de tiempo* porque puedes aprender mucho.

c Me gustaría ser médico o veterinario, pero *afortunadamente / desafortunadamente* no saco buenas notas en ciencias.

d Hacer un curso de primeros auxilios es *una buena idea / una mala idea* para los que hacen de canguro.

e *Admiro / No aguanto* a los que trabajan de bomberos o policías porque son valientes y ayudan a la gente.

3 Practice finding opinions and justifications in a text. Read what Miguel says about his job. Highlight (✐) the reasons or examples given in the text for each of the following statements.

Creo que tengo mucha suerte porque tengo un trabajo que me encanta. Me chifla el deporte y soy profesor de educación física. Lo que más me gusta es ver cómo los chicos se divierten cuando hacen deporte y cómo aprenden a trabajar en equipo y llevarse bien con sus compañeros. Además, pienso que la actividad física ayuda a los jóvenes a estudiar mejor y a tener más confianza en sí mismos. El aspecto negativo es que siempre hay algunos estudiantes que no quieren trabajar, pero afortunadamente, son una minoría.

a He thinks he's lucky.

b The thing he likes most about his job.

c What physical activity does for young people.

d The example he gives of a negative aspect of his work.

3 **How do I answer questions by combining information from different parts of a text?**

You need to read all of the text in an exam task to make sure you can answer the questions correctly. Read texts and questions carefully to find the clues and connections to help you answer accurately.

① Read the introduction and timetable below. Then look at the questions that follow and make notes 🖋 in each box.

Estás mirando los planes de tu amigo, Pablo, antes de su entrevista de trabajo.

sábado	Ir al centro comercial – comprar traje nuevo
domingo	Investigación sobre la empresa
lunes	Escribe preguntas para hacer en la entrevista
martes	Busca información sobre la ruta y los autobuses
miércoles	Piensa en típicas preguntas de entrevista y considera respuestas
jueves	Plancha la camisa y limpia los zapatos

Notice that the questions do not usually use the same vocabulary as the text. You need to use your knowledge of synonyms to arrive at the right answer. (See p. 20 for the section on synonyms). To practise this skill, scan the information provided, eliminate the sections that are irrelevant until you are left with the correct answer.

Example: ¿Qué día prepara Pablo la ropa para la entrevista?

Which two entries refer to clothes (ropa)?	Which of the two entries talks about buying clothes?	The answer to the question is:
sábado + jueves	sábado	jueves

a ¿Qué día planea Pablo su viaje a la entrevista?

Which two entries refer to going somewhere?	Which of the two entries talks about <u>going shopping</u>?	The answer to the question is:

b ¿Qué día se informará Pablo sobre la compañía?

Which two entries refer to finding information?	Which of the two entries talks about <u>transport information</u>?	The answer to the question is:

c ¿Qué día pensará Pablo en preguntas que puede usar en la entrevista?

Which two entries refer to questions?	Which of the two entries talks about questions likely <u>to be asked</u> at interview?	The answer to the question is:

Your turn!

Here is an exam-style question for you to practise the skills you have worked on, specifically how to show that you can use ideas and information to make connections between different parts of a text. ✏

Taking a gap year

You read this article on a Spanish website.

Tomarse un año sabático empieza a ser una práctica más común en España. Al terminar los estudios en el instituto, muchos jóvenes no saben qué estudiar en la universidad; pasar un año fuera del sistema educativo les ofrece enriquecedoras oportunidades.

Isabel Hernández, 18 años y de Madrid, nos dijo que fue a estudiar inglés a Australia durante un año. Ahora ha vuelto e irá a la Universidad a estudiar arquitectura. Dice que la experiencia le ayudó a mejorar su nivel de inglés y a ser más independiente y más responsable.

"Tomarse un año para trabajar y visitar otro país trae ventajas," dice María Luisa Bertrán, profesora de psicología. "Conocer otras culturas ayuda a los jóvenes. Aprenden a comunicarse y a adaptarse mejor, a trabajar en equipo y, quizás la habilidad más importante en el mundo del trabajo hoy en día, a tener una perspectiva más abierta del mundo."

Answer the following questions **in English**.

1   Is taking a gap year a long-established tradition in Spain?

Yes ☐ No ☐ Give a reason for your answer.

.... **(1 mark)**

2   What did Isabel Hernández gain from her gap year?

.... **(1 mark)**

3   What would be most valued by employers?

.... **(1 mark)**

Notice that the answer to **1** is not given directly in the text. Look at the first sentence of the text and work out what it implies about gap years in Spain.

To be able to answer **3**, you need to sift through a number of valuable skills to find the right one that exactly answers the question.

Your turn!

Here is an exam-style question for you to practise the skills you have worked on, specifically how to identify opinions and justifications. 🖉

Exam-style question

Student jobs

You read this extract from a web page about jobs for students.

> Muchas tiendas de ropa tienen vacantes durante los meses de julio y agosto. Se necesita gente para trabajar durante el verano para sustituir a los dependientes que se van de vacaciones. Debes tener buena presencia y la habilidad de comunicarte con los clientes. Saber hablar inglés, francés o alemán sería una ventaja. Lo bueno: recibirás descuentos (podrás comprar, por ejemplo, ropa a precios reducidos). Lo malo: tendrás que trabajar los fines de semana.
>
> En Cinemundo, hay trabajo durante todo el año para jóvenes y estudiantes. Debes tener 16 años o más. Trabajarás sólo 4 horas al día y cambiarás de tarea cada día. Un día venderás entradas, al día siguiente venderás refrescos y dulces, y así sucesivamente. El trabajo es variado y puedes ver las películas gratis, pero el sueldo es bajo.

Answer the following questions **in English**.

1 What would you be doing if you applied for the first job mentioned?

.... **(1 mark)**

2 Why are extra staff needed at this time of year?

.... **(1 mark)**

3 What is the advantage of this type of summer job?

.... **(1 mark)**

4 Who can apply for the cinema job?

.... **(1 mark)**

5 What is the disadvantage of working in Cinemundo?

.... **(1 mark)**

Notice that you will need to infer what is implied in the text to answer the first question. The text tells you the job title and the place, so from that you have to infer what the work would be.

Look for words and phrases that introduce positive and negative ideas. These will help you to find the answers about the advantages and disadvantages of the jobs.

Review your skills

Check up

Review your responses to the exam-style questions on pages 55 and 56. Tick ✓ the column that shows how well you think you have done each of the following.

	Not quite ✓	Nearly there ✓	Got it! ✓
recognised positive and negative ideas	☐	☐	☐
identified opinions and justifications	☐	☐	☐
answered questions by combining information from different parts of the text	☐	☐	☐

Need more practice?

Go back to pages 50 and 51 and complete 🖉 the two exam-style questions there. Use the checklist to help you.

Checklist In my answers, do I ...	✓
identify words and phrases that express ideas, thoughts and opinions?	
recognise words and phrases that introduce a positive or negative opinion?	
identify words and phrases that imply opinions?	
use inference to understand implied meaning?	
use information from different parts of the texts to infer meaning?	

> Remember that, in reading tasks, the questions and the text use different words and phrases to refer to the same ideas and information. Knowing the vocabulary for each topic will help you to identify the connections and the meaning.

How confident do you feel about each of these **skills**? Colour in 🖉 the bars.

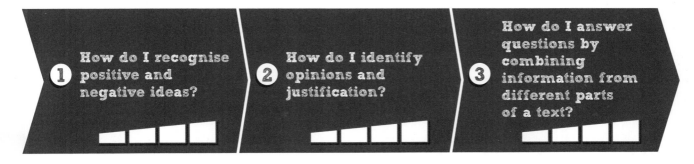

1 How do I recognise positive and negative ideas?

2 How do I identify opinions and justification?

3 How do I answer questions by combining information from different parts of a text?

8 Translating accurately into English

This unit will help you to improve your accuracy when translating from Spanish into English. The skills you will build are to:

- make sure you include all key details
- avoid including superfluous material
- avoid distorting the meaning of sentences.

In the exam, you will be asked to do a translation task similar to the ones on these two pages. This unit will prepare you to tackle translating carefully and accurately.

> The key to getting good marks in a passage like this is to look carefully at the detail and to make sure you include it all in your translation. Look at the verbs to get the tense right (present, past, future). Look at the adjectives: *un pueblo pequeño, el viaje largo*. Make sure you include all the information. In this passage, for example, include all the family members mentioned: *mis padres, mi hermana, mis tíos, mis primos*.

Do not answer this question yet. You will be asked to come back to it at the end of the unit.

Exam-style question

You see this post on Facebook. Translate it **into English** for your family.

> Vivo en un pueblo pequeño en el norte de España. Me gusta nadar y me gusta la gimnasia. El año pasado fui de vacaciones a Francia con mis padres, mi hermana, mis tíos y mis primos. Fuimos en coche y el viaje fue bastante largo, pero lo pasamos muy bien. Este año, iré a un campamento de verano en las montañas con mi hermana.

(9 marks)

....

....

....

....

....

....

....

....

Do not answer this question yet. You will be asked to come back to it at the end of the unit.

Exam-style question

Your Spanish friend emails you about a charity event. Translate it **into English** for your family.

> En febrero, organizamos una carrera solidaria en bici en mi pueblo. Participaron más de cincuenta personas. Hacía bastante frío y hacía viento pero, a pesar del mal tiempo, lo pasamos bien. Después desayunamos todos en el bar del pueblo. Vamos a repetir la carrera el año que viene.

(9 marks)

....

....

....

....

....

(1) Read the exam-style question and look at a student's English translation. He has made several mistakes. Look through the comments. Underline (A) the problems in his text.

- Verb tense is incorrect (–ar verbs have the same form for 'we' plural in the present and the preterite, so you need to look at other verbs to see if they're in the past or present, e.g. *participaron*).

- A word (*charity*) is missing, so not all the information is given.

- An unknown expression, which could have been understood in context, was left out.

In February, we are organising a bike race in my village.

- **a** They took part more of 50 people.

- **b** It was quite cold and it was windy, but we had a good time.

- **c** Afterwards, we all had breakfast in the bar of the village.

- **d** We are going to do the race again the year coming.

- The word order in the sentence is not correct in English.

- An expression is translated word for word and does not make sense in English.

- An expression is translated word for word and does not sound natural in English.

- An expression is translated word for word and does not sound natural in English.

The three key questions in the **skills boosts** will help you to improve how you answer these types of questions.

1 How do I ensure that I have included all key elements?

2 How do I avoid including superfluous material?

3 How do I avoid distorting the meaning of sentences?

1 **How do I ensure that I have included all key elements?**

To make sure you include all the key elements, you must check that every piece of information in the Spanish text appears in your translation.

- Look for **time expressions** in texts and make sure you include them in your translation.
- Also, make sure you include the phrases that tell you **how often** something happens such as *a veces, siempre, generalmente, de vez en cuando, casi nunca.*
- Remember to translate '**intensifiers**' (words such as *muy, mucho, más, bastante, demasiado,* etc.)

① Highlight ⟨✐⟩ the word or expression in each Spanish sentence that is missed out in the English translation. Then add ⟨✐⟩ the missing words or expressions to the English translation.

a El ciclismo es muy popular ahora. *Cycling is very popular^.*

                                                              now

b Fuimos de excursión a las montañas hace dos semanas.

    We went on a trip to the mountains.

c En las grandes ciudades hay demasiada gente sin techo.

    In the big cities there are homeless people.

d Beber demasiado alcohol es un problema bastante serio.

    Drinking too much alcohol is a serious problem.

② Read a student's translation of the text in the exam-style question. Compare the translation with the text. There are six details missing.

> You have received this post on Facebook. Translate **into English** for your friend.
>
> > Me encanta el deporte y normalmente practico algún deporte casi todos los días. Casi nunca veo la tele porque es aburrido, pero hace poco vi un campeonato de atletismo en que una atleta de mi región ganó una medalla. Fue muy emocionante. El año que viene me gustaría participar en un triatlón.

                            usually
I love sport and I ^ do some kind of sport every day. I never watch TV because it's

boring, but I watched an athletics championship in which an athlete from my area won

a medal. It was exciting. I would like to take part in a triathlon.

a Highlight ⟨✐⟩ the six words or phrases in the Spanish text that are not included in the English translation.

b Show where the details should appear in the English translation and write ⟨✐⟩ them in.

❷ How do I avoid including superfluous material?

Although you know that languages cannot be translated word for word and that you need to think of the English equivalent of Spanish expressions, you must be careful not to add words or phrases in your translation that aren't necessary in English.

In Spanish, the definite article (*el, la, los, las*) is used much more than the English word 'the'.

① Read the Spanish sentences and strikethrough ~~cat~~ the words in the English translations that are unnecessary. On paper, rewrite ✏ the ones that need to change the word order.

a Creo que el problema más preocupante es el calentamiento global.

I think that the most worrying problem is ~~the~~ climate change.

b Hay que proteger los bosques.

We must protect the tropical forests.

c Debemos animar a todos a reciclar más.

We should encourage to everyone to recycle more.

d Voy al instituto en bici o a pie todos los días.

I go to the school by bike or on foot every day.

e La contaminación del aire es un problema grave en las grandes ciudades.

The pollution of the air in the big cities is a serious problem.

f El coche de mi padre es eléctrico.

The car of my father is electric.

② Read the sentences in Spanish and write ✏ a word or words in the gaps to complete the English translations.

a Vivo en una ciudad industrial al norte de Barcelona.

I live in an industrial city .... *Barcelona.*

b El problema del medio ambiente que más me preocupa es la contaminación del aire.

The environmental problem that worries me most is ....

c Hay demasiados coches y camiones en el centro de la ciudad.

There are too many cars and lorries in ....

d Debemos usar el transporte público o ir a pie.

We should use .... *or go on foot.*

e Hay que informar al público de la importancia de cuidar el medio ambiente.

We must inform .... *the importance of looking after the environment.*

3 **How do I avoid distorting the meaning of sentences?**

Wrongly translating a word or phrase can change the meaning of a sentence, so you need to be as accurate as possible. Focus on the words and phrases you know and keep guesswork to a minimum.

1 **a** Read the Spanish text. A student has translated it, but has left gaps because she didn't know some of the words. Highlight 🖉 the words in the Spanish text which haven't been translated.

> En casa hacemos todo lo posible para ahorrar energía. En invierno, sólo usamos la calefacción cuando hace mucho frío. En verano, cerramos las cortinas y las persianas durante el día y la casa se queda fresca por dentro. De esta manera, usamos los ventiladores únicamente cuando hace mucho calor. Además, tenemos placas solares en el techo para calentar el agua.

> At home we do everything we can to save energy. In winter, we only use the
>
> i .... when it's very cold. In summer, we close the curtains and the
>
> ii .... during the day and the house stays cool inside. This way,
>
> we only use the iii .... when it's very hot.
>
> In addition, we have iv .... on the v .... to heat the water.

b Read the English translation again and choose the option for each gap in **1**. Look at the context each time to see which word makes most sense. Note down 🖉 what helped you to decide.

i	cooker	gas fire	heating	*We only use it when it's cold.*
ii	windows	blinds	carpets	....
iii	fans	radiators	freezer	....
iv	sunshades	solar panels	double glazing	....
v	garden	terrace	roof	....

> If you have to guess the meaning of a word or phrase, look at the sentence in your translation and ask yourself 'Does this make sense?'

2 Highlight 🖉 the words or phrases that are incorrectly translated in these sentences. (**Clue:** they don't make sense!) Then correct 🖉 them, as in the example.

Example: Tener una dieta sana y hacer deporte es importante para la salud.

  Going on a ~~crazy~~ diet and doing sport is important for good health. <u>healthy</u>

a Voy a comer más ensalada, verduras y fruta.

  I'm going to eat more salad, leaves and fruit. ....

b Me gustan las manzanas, pero no me gustan las peras.

  I like apples, but I don't like hot dogs. ....

c Vivimos en un barrio en las afueras de la ciudad y hay mucho tráfico.

  We live in a bar in the outskirts of the city and there is a lot of traffic. ....

d Hay que apagar las luces para ahorrar energía.

  We must switch on the lights to save energy. ....

Your turn!

Here is an exam-style question for you to practise the skills you have worked on, specifically how to include all the key details. 🖉

- Read through the Spanish text before you translate it to get a general idea of what it's about.
- Then look at each sentence.
- Break each sentence down into phrases and work out what they mean and how you express them in English.

Exam-style question

You've seen this text on a news website. Translate it **into English** for your friend.

> Pienso que los atletas paralímpicos son buenos modelos a seguir para los niños y los jóvenes porque luchan para superar muchas dificultades. Además, creo que vale la pena participar en eventos solidarios. Hace poco, trabajé como voluntario en una carrera ciclista en mi región que recaudó fondos para los sin techo. Fue una experiencia muy positiva.

(9 marks)

....

....

....

....

....

....

....

....

Remember that in Spanish, the words for 'the' (*el, la, los, las*) are used more than in English. When translating a passage like this one, think of how we would express the same phrases in English. Take the first sentence in the passage, for example. The words for 'the' are not needed in English in the first sentence (*los atletas, los niños, los jóvenes*).

Learning whole phrases that put vocabulary into context will help you with translating from Spanish. Look at the passage here and identify all the phrases you know and can translate easily before you start to write your translation.

Your turn!

Here is an exam-style question for you to practise the skills you have worked on, specifically how to avoid including superfluous material and how to avoid distorting the meaning of sentences. ✎

Exam-style question

You have seen this blog by your Spanish friend. Translate it **into English** for your parents.

> Hace dos meses, cambié de trabajo y ahora no tengo tiempo para ir al gimnasio ni a la piscina. Para relajarme, empecé a fumar, pero ahora necesito cambiar mi rutina para llevar una vida sana. Creo que, de lunes a viernes, voy a levantarme más temprano para correr antes de ir a la oficina. Voy a cambiar mi dieta y comer más ensalada, verduras y fruta. Además, voy a dejar de fumar.

(9 marks)

....

....

....

....

....

....

....

....

To avoid writing English that sounds unnatural, remember to ask yourself: 'How would you say this in English?'

Be careful when you translate false friends! For example, *una vida sana* because *sana* means 'healthy' not 'sane'.

Review your skills

Check up

Review your responses to the exam-style questions on pages 63 and 64. Tick ⊘ the column that shows how well you think you have done each of the following.

	Not quite ⊘	Nearly there ⊘	Got it! ⊘
made sure I included all key details	☐	☐	☐
avoided including superfluous material	☐	☐	☐
avoided distorting the meaning of sentences	☐	☐	☐

Need more practice?

Go back to pages 58 and 59 and complete ⊘ the two exam-style questions there. Use the checklist to help you.

Checklist In my answers, do I ...	⊘
include all the information that's in the Spanish text?	
identify and translate the verb tenses correctly?	
identify and translate the time expressions?	
identify and translate the intensifiers (*muy, mucho*, etc.)?	
avoid putting words and information that don't appear in the Spanish text or that aren't necessary in English?	
keep guesswork to a minimum to avoid distorting the meaning of the text?	
consider how Spanish words and phrases are expressed in English to avoid translating word for word?	

How confident do you feel about each of these **skills**? Colour in ⊘ the bars.

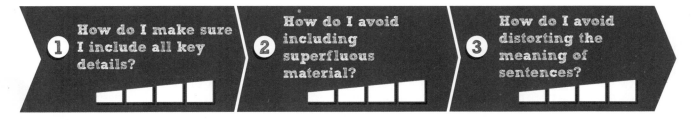

1 How do I make sure I include all key details?

2 How do I avoid including superfluous material?

3 How do I avoid distorting the meaning of sentences?

9 Using different clues to understand unfamiliar language

This unit will help you to deal with unfamiliar words and phrases. The skills you will build are to:

- use clues from the rubrics, headings and text
- use clues from the text surrounding unfamiliar words
- recognise parts of unfamiliar words.

The level of the language and tasks in this unit is a little higher than in the other units, so it will prepare you to tackle Higher level questions.

Do not answer this question yet. You will be asked to come back to it at the end of the unit.

Exam-style question

An interview with my grandmother

Read what the writer's grandmother said about changes in her lifetime.

> Mi abuela se llama Carmen. Nació en los años cuarenta, una época muy distinta a la nuestra. En aquel entonces, muchos jóvenes solían dejar la escuela a los 14 años para empezar a trabajar. Mi abuela trabajaba limpiando casas desde los 14 años hasta que se casó a los 20 años. Luego se ocupó de la casa y de los niños. Dice que su generación tenía menos oportunidades, pero que la vida era más sencilla y más tranquila. Se queja de la falta de respeto de la juventud actual. Según ella, antes se respetaba más a los padres y a los profesores. "Cuando te regañaban por algo, te regañaban mucho y tenías miedo. Ahora, los chicos ni hacen caso."
>
> Cuando mi abuela era joven, su familia no disponía de teléfono, ni televisor, ni lavadora. Desde niña, tenía que ayudar con todas las tareas. En el tiempo libre, se escuchaba la radio y se cosía. Después de comer, se echaba la siesta y luego, recuerda mi abuela que solía sentarse con su madre y sus vecinas en el patio a coser, a bordar y a charlar. Cosían y bordaban ropa para los niños, además de cosas para la casa.

Answer the following questions **in English**.

1 When was the writer's grandmother born?

.... (1 mark)

2 What was the school leaving age then?

.... (1 mark)

3 What did Carmen do after she was married?

.... (1 mark)

4 What is wrong with young people today, according to Carmen?

.... (1 mark)

5 What did Carmen and her mother used to make while sitting on the patio?

.... (1 mark)

Do not answer this question yet. You will be asked to come back to it at the end of the unit.

Exam-style question

Las preocupaciones para el futuro

Ves este artículo en una página web española.

Párrafo A	Si el ser humano va a sobrevivir, ha de ser optimista y actuar para resolver los problemas más serios. En cuanto al medio ambiente, creo que lo más preocupante es el cambio climático porque será irreversible. Provocará sequías e inundaciones y convertirá muchas regiones del mundo en lugares inhabitables.
Párrafo B	La escasez de agua, en un futuro bastante cercano, presentará un problema enorme para el mundo. Algunos expertos dicen que será el recurso más valioso a finales de este siglo.
Párrafo C	Debemos buscar soluciones para los millones de personas desplazadas por conflictos como guerras civiles y por desastres naturales. Es uno de los problemas más graves que tendrá que enfrentar nuestra generación y es imprescindible solucionarlo.
Párrafo D	Acabo de leer que, a pesar de las campañas medioambientales, la cantidad de basura en las grandes ciudades del mundo está aumentando y que se duplicará dentro de diez años. ¡Qué horror! Tenemos que reciclar todo lo posible y reducir la cantidad de material que tiramos.

¿En qué párrafo se encuentran las opiniones siguientes? Escribe la letra correcta en cada casilla.

Ejemplo: 'El hombre debe tomar medidas positivas para proteger el futuro del planeta.' `A`

1 'En el futuro habrá una falta de un recurso esencial para nuestra supervivencia.' ☐ (1 mark)

2 'Los cambios en el tiempo causarán efectos extremos y devastadores.' ☐ (1 mark)

3 'He visto una predicción alarmante que afectará a las poblaciones urbanas.' ☐ (1 mark)

4 'Es fundamental encontrar maneras de enfrentar las migraciones masivas.' ☐ (1 mark)

5 'Habrá zonas donde ya no será posible vivir.' ☐ (1 mark)

> Texts about the environment and global issues can look complex and daunting but international topics such as these often use terms that are cognates or near-cognates of the equivalent terms in English.

The three key questions in the **skills boosts** will help you to improve how you answer these types of question.

1 How do I use clues from the rubrics, headings and text?

2 How do I use clues from the text surrounding unfamiliar words?

3 How do I recognise parts of unfamiliar words?

How do I use clues from the rubrics, headings and text?

The heading above a reading task tells you what the text is about. The rubric (instruction line) underneath the heading gives you more information. Read these carefully to establish what the context of the text is before you start to read it. Knowing the context makes it easier to work out the meaning of unfamiliar words and phrases.

① Read the headings and the rubrics from exam texts. Highlight 🖉 the words that are the key to the context of each text, as in the example.

Example: Work experience

You see these advertisements on a website for jobs in Spain.

ⓐ **Protege tu planeta**

Ves los consejos para cuidar el medio ambiente en una página web española.

ⓑ **Un año académico en Canadá**

Lee sobre la experiencia de un estudiante español en el extranjero.

ⓒ *Manolito Gafotas* by Elvira Lindo

Read the text about Manolito's day out in Madrid with his grandfather.

ⓓ **¿Se puede vivir sin el móvil?**

Ves este artículo sobre cómo la tecnología móvil nos cambia la vida.

② ⓐ Read the extracts and circle Ⓐ the most likely meaning of the highlighted words.

ⓑ On paper, explain 🖉 how you worked out the answers. Look at the example to help you.

> **Twenty practical tips for protecting the environment**
> Las bombillas LED son de bajo consumo de energía y duran mucho más que las bombillas tradicionales.

Example: *batteries* (*light bulbs*) *fridges*

The heading mentions protecting the environment and the text in Spanish says that 'bombillas' LED
use less energy, so 'light bulbs' is the most likely meaning

> **Evento deportivo solidario**
> Participa en una caminata nocturna de 5K a la luz de la luna para recaudar fondos para el Hospital de niños.

i *concert*   *night shift*   *night walk*

> **Un año académico en Canadá**
> Mejoré mi nivel de inglés porque estudié en un colegio público y conviví con una familia canadiense.

ii *got to know*   *lived with*   *studied with*

> **La tecnología móvil es imprescindible**
> Si nos encontramos en un sitio muy apartado donde no hay cobertura y no funciona el móvil, sufrimos un ataque de nervios.

iii *there's no shelter*   *there's no electricity*   *there's no signal*

2 How do I use clues from the text surrounding unfamiliar words?

When you find a word in a sentence that you don't know, look at the words around it for clues. This will give you an idea of the meaning. Use the tips in the hint box to help you.

A Look for words you already know in Spanish.

B Look at the verbs and the tenses used.

C Look for words that are the same or similar in English (cognates and near-cognates).

D Look at the words that surround the cognates to see what they connect with.

E Look for words that are based on words you might already know in Spanish (e.g. *entretener* to entertain, *olvidar* to forget).

1 Read the sentences and circle (A) the words which give you clues to the meaning of the highlighted words. Write (✏) the letter of the tip from the hint box that helped you.

a La (canción), *Despacito*, ha sido el (número uno) en las listas de éxito en más de ochenta países del mundo. | A |

b El guion de la película estaba mal escrito, pero por lo menos los actores eran buenos. | |

c Fuimos a un partido en el Camp Nou y el ambiente en el estadio era fantástico. | |

d Para ir a la boda de mi prima, tuve que llevar traje y corbata. | |

e No ha sido una serie de televisión de alta calidad, pero ha sido muy entretenida. | |

f La música de las bandas sonoras de *Gladiador y El Señor de los Anillos* ha llegado a ser música clásica de cine. | |

g Según una encuesta reciente, un 60% de los españoles no ha leído *Don Quijote*. | |

2 Using the clues you have circled in **1**, read the sentences above again and underline (A) the correct meaning of the highlighted words.

a (las listas de éxito)   sales lists   record charts   discotheques

b (guión)   script   casting   special effects

c (ambiente)   atmosphere   noise   exciting

d (boda)   birthday party   house   wedding

e (entretenida)   entertaining   boring   disappointing

f (las bandas sonoras)   bands   sound effects   soundtracks

g (según)   despite   although   according to

To make sure your answer is correct, go back and check that the meaning you chose makes sense in the sentence.

③ How do I recognise parts of unfamiliar words?

Looking very carefully at individual words can help you understand their meaning by:

- learning the meaning of common beginnings and endings (prefixes and suffixes)
- spotting the main word within a word (root).

① Look at the words in bold in these sentences about learning a language abroad. Use the table of prefixes to help you work out the meaning of the words in English and write 🖉 them on paper.

Example: 1 inter/actuar = interact, operate together

a Sobretodo debes **interactuar** y **convivir** con los demás estudiantes, de esta manera no **malgastarás el** tiempo. No es **imposible** hacer nuevos amigos en el extranjero.

b Es fácil **prever** las dificultades: **malentender** lo que te dicen es normal. Por lo general, la gente no es **impaciente** si no comprendes inmediatamente.

Prefixes	Meaning
ante-	before
con-/com-/co-	with, together
des-	un- / dis-
im-/in-	opposite
inter-	inside, among, between, together
mal-	bad / badly
pre-	pre- / fore-

c **Desafortunadamente**, a veces hay problemas: **anteayer** era **incapaz** de interrumpir a un amigo que hablaba muy rápido.

② Look at the words in bold in these sentences. Look at the table to help you work out the meaning of the suffix and, on paper, write 🖉 down the meaning of the words in English.

Example: panadero = baker (occupation)

a El **panadero** era muy **hablador** y un **simpaticón**. Su **panadería** estaba en una **callecita encantadora** que pasábamos **frecuentemente**.

b La **lavadora** no funciona, no encuentro el **secador** y tengo que pasar la **aspiradora** por el **comedor**.

c Para mí es importante hacer trabajo **voluntario**. Me gustaría participar en un proyecto **medioambiental**.

Suffixes	Meaning, use
diminutives	
-ito/-ita, -illo/-illa	little/dear
augmentatives	
-ote /-ota, -ón/ona	big, negative
-ante	verb → noun / adjective
-dor/-dora, -tor/-tora, -sor/-sora	verb → occupations, places
-al	noun → adjective
-ario/-aria	profession, place, '-ary'
-ero/era, -ista	occupation, 'related to'

③ Look at these words and highlight 🖉 the root as in the example and try and work out the meaning of each word. Write 🖉 the root word in column A and the translation in column B.

	A	B
irrepetible	repetir	unrepeatable
subalimentación		
desordenadamente		
agrandamiento		
aconsejar		
entremetido		
desilusionante		

Many words are made up of a root plus a suffix and even a prefix: *desproporcionado* = disproportionate. Note that the root word may be slightly modified but it will still be recognisable.

Your turn!

Here is an exam-style question which requires you to put into practice the skills you have worked on, specifically how to make use of the general context and that of the words around the difficult words. ✎

Exam-style question

Volunteering abroad

Read what Nuria has written about her volunteering experiences with a humanitarian charity.

> He estado en Cuba haciendo trabajo voluntario para una ONG que se ocupa del bienestar de la gente más necesitada en los suburbios de La Habana. Llevé donaciones, por ejemplo, pasta de dientes, jabón, maquinillas de afeitar – productos de primera necesidad a los que nosotros estamos muy acostumbrados, pero que en Cuba no son tan fáciles de conseguir. A través de los artículos donados y la ayuda práctica de algunos voluntarios cubanos, la ONG consigue apoyar a personas como Enrique, de 92 años, que no puede salir de su casa por no tener una silla de ruedas. Aunque la pobreza es patente, sorprende la generosidad de los cubanos, que ponen su granito de arena para hacer más tolerable la vida de los desdichados.

Answer the following questions **in English**.

1 What is the work of the charity Nuria volunteered with?

.... (1 mark)

2 Why did the charity need the items Nuria took with her?

.... (1 mark)

3 How does the charity help people?

.... (1 mark)

4 Why couldn't Enrique leave his house?

.... (1 mark)

5 What did Nuria find surprising?

.... (1 mark)

- Use the context: look for clues in the heading or in the instructions. The heading and instruction for this question indicate that you can expect to read a person's description of working in a team engaged in some sort of community action in another country.
- Look for clues to understand difficult words in the sentence, for example, an *explanation*. Look for commas, brackets or dashes to indicate an explanation. In the second sentence, the dash after the examples of the donations Nuria took with her will provide you with the answer to **2**.
- Look out for words and phrases that introduce contrasting information such as *aunque* and *al contrario*, as they can help you work out the meaning.

Your turn!

Here is another exam-style question which requires you to put into practice the skills you have worked on, particularly how to look carefully at the beginning, middle and end of difficult words to find clues to their meaning. 🖉

Exam-style question

Taking a Gap Year

Read this article that your Mexican friend points out to you on a website.

> Viajar sola es una de las mejores experiencias que he tenido, pues se vive todo mucho más intensamente. Estando lejos valoras todo mucho más, especialmente a los seres queridos que están lejos. Te das cuenta que la distancia no puede separarte de ellos. También, viajando te das cuenta de la cruda realidad de cómo está el mundo. He visto mucha pobreza, familias que viven con escasos recursos, personas desgastadas trabajando más de catorce horas diarias, niños que en vez de ir al colegio mendigan por las calles… Son cosas que no ves en los medios de comunicación.
>
> Mi nivel de inglés ha sido siempre bastante bueno, pero aun así, me queda muchísimo por aprender y esto de viajar me ha acelerado el proceso de aprendizaje. Es el idioma por el cual los mochileros se comunican y, sobretodo, hablándolo te haces amigos de todo el mundo.

You might not know the word *mendigar* (to beg), but you might be able to deduce its meaning from the context of poverty and the rest of the sentence.

Are you unsure about the meaning of the word *mochileros*? Look for the root of the word.

Answer the following questions **in English**.

1 Who did the writer miss on her travels?

.... (1 mark)

2 What shocked the writer about the working conditions of some people?

.... (1 mark)

3 What does she mention about the children she saw?

.... (1 mark)

4 Why do people in general not get to see these things?

.... (1 mark)

5 Why did she manage to improve her English on her travels?

.... (1 mark)

Review your skills

Check up

Review your responses to the exam-style questions on pages 71 and 72. Tick ✓ the column that shows how well you think you have done each of the following.

	Not quite ✓	Nearly there ✓	Got it! ✓
used clues from the rubrics, headings and text	☐	☐	☐
used clues from the text surrounding unfamiliar words	☐	☐	☐
recognised parts of the unfamiliar words	☐	☐	☐

Need more practice?

Go back to pages 66 and 67 and complete 🖉 the two exam-style questions there. Use the checklist to help you.

Checklist In my answers, do I...	✓
read the rubrics and the headings to find information that will help me understand the text?	
look for words I already know in Spanish surrounding the words I don't know?	
look for cognates and near-cognates?	
work out the meaning of unfamiliar words because they're based on words I already know?	
look at the roots, prefixes and suffixes of unfamiliar words to work out their meaning?	

How confident do you feel about each of these **skills**? Colour in 🖉 the bars.

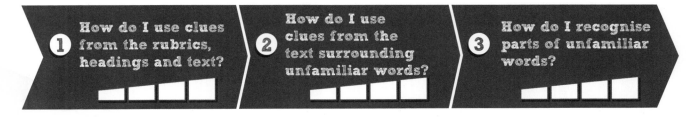

1. How do I use clues from the rubrics, headings and text?

2. How do I use clues from the text surrounding unfamiliar words?

3. How do I recognise parts of unfamiliar words?

Answers

Unit 1

Page 2

① (circled)

Prefiero

me encanta

Me gustan

No me interesa

Me encanta

Me fascinan

Para mí es (importante)

Es (divertido)

Page 3

② Places: castillo, puente romano, playa

Activities: comprar comida / regalos, tomar un refresco / el sol

Page 4

① ⓐ i D; ii H; iii K; iv B; v I; vi F; vii J; viii G; ix A; x C; xi L; xii E

ⓑ i viajar

ii castillo

iii comprar

iv coche

v perder

② ⓐ i D barato

ii A tren, miedo, volar

iii E frío, nieve, esquiar

iv C amigos, divertido

ⓑ i D

ii A

iii E

iv C

Page 5

① ⓐ and ⓑ

ii partido – sports match, comprar – buy, entradas – tickets

iii comprar – buy, crema solar – sun protection, playa – beach, quemarse – burn

iv perder – loose, pasaporte & cartera – passport and wallet (valuables), desastre – disaster (negative reaction)

v alojamiento – lodging, piscina & restaurantes – swimming pool and restaurant (amenities)

vi plan & folleto – map and brochure (tourist information), lugares de interés – touristy places

ⓒ A iii, B ii, C i, D vi, E iv, F v

Page 6

① ⓐ i A for B to, ii A through B by, iii A from B of, iv A in B on

② ⓐ ii asisto, 'to attend', principiantes, 'beginners'

ⓑ i una hora, the indefinite article 'an' + the word for 'hour', not 'time'

ⓒ i me, the first person pronoun that goes with the verb for 'to love'

ⓓ ii tienen, the third person plural of a verb, plural of adjective 'nuevo'

Page 7

Exam-style question

1 A, 2 D, 3 E, 4 C

Page 8

Exam-style question

1 clothes shop (E) 2 supermarket (B) 3 bike hire shop (G) 4 museum (C) 5 garage (F)

Page 9

Page 2 Exam-style question

1 B, 2 C, 3 A, 4 E

Page 3 Exam-style question

Plan 1 – C

Plan 2 – F

Plan 3 – A

Plan 4 – G

Unit 2

Page 11

① cognates: gimnasio, universidad, frustración, problema, condiciones, excepción, estricto, humor, excursiones, manera

There are also near-cognates: adecuadas, equipado, estudiar, laboratorios, organiza

False friends: instituto, instalaciones, antiguos, profesor/profesores, simpáticos

Page 12

② ⓐ club, judo, opinión, participar, competiciones, nacionales, parte, actividad, noviembre, trofeo

ⓑ uniforme, formal, limita, individualidad, práctico, diferencias, económicas, estudiantes, obvias

ⓒ necesarias, ejemplo, permite, usar, móvil, clase, prohibido, agresivo, grosero, puntual

③ (a) and (b)

i foto – photo, gimnasia – gymnastics

ii geografia – geography, estudiamos – study, contaminación – contamination, reciclaje – recycling

iii excursión – excursion, estadio – stadium, olímpicos – olympics

iv trofeo – trophy, esquí – skiing

v estrés – stress, fenomenal – phenomenal

Page 13

① (a) i 6 El profesor de <u>educación</u> de <u>física</u> es <u>estricto</u>, no tiene <u>paciencia</u> pero <u>controla</u> bien la <u>clase</u>.

ii 4 Tengo que <u>admitir</u> que me gusta <u>estudiar</u> la <u>historia</u> y la <u>geografía</u>.

iii 3 <u>Normalmente</u> voy al <u>club</u> de <u>fotogafía</u> los lunes.

iv 3 Después de mi <u>experiencia</u>, no puedo <u>decidir</u> si voy a <u>participar</u> otra vez.

v 3 <u>Desafortunadamente</u> el <u>uniforme</u> de mi colegio <u>primario</u> en <u>primaria</u> era feo.

vi 4 Para hacer esta <u>actividad</u> es <u>necesario</u> poner <u>atención</u> y aprender el <u>vocabulario.</u>

vii 3 En mi instituto no hay mucha <u>intimidación</u> ni <u>violencia</u> entre los <u>estudiantes</u>.

viii 3 Tengo la <u>oportunidad</u> de <u>participar</u> en un intercambio y <u>visitar</u> a mi amigo español.

ix 4 Estoy <u>estudiando</u> para el <u>examen</u> de <u>biología</u>. Tengo que escribir sobre un <u>experimento</u>.

x 3 Mi compañero no es <u>estúpido</u>, es muy <u>inteligente</u> pero es muy <u>tímido</u>.

(b) i The PE (physical education) teacher is strict; he has no patience, but he controls the class well.

ii I have to admit that I like studying history and geography.

iii Normally, I go to the photography club on Mondays.

iv After my experience, I cannot decide if I'm going to participate again.

v Unfortunately, the uniform in my primary school was ugly.

vi In order to do this activity it's necessary to pay attention and learn the vocabulary.

vii In my school there isn't much intimidation/ bullying or violence among the students.

viii I have the opportunity to participate in an exchange and visit my Spanish friend.

ix I am studying for the biology exam. I have to write about an experiment.

x My classmate isn't stupid, he's very intelligent but he's timid/shy.

②

Spanish	English	Examples from sentences
<u>Changes on word endings</u>: Verbs Ending in consonant, add –ar or -ir		controlar/control admitir/admit visitar/visit
-ar or -ir	-e	decidir/decide admitir/admit participar/participate
nouns or adjectives in -encia	-ence	violencia/violence paciencia /pacience
-ario	-ary	necesario/necessary vocabulario/vocabulary primaria/primary
-ción	-tion	intimidación/intimidate atención/attention educación/education
-dad	-ty	oportunidad/ opportunity actividad/activity
-ía/-ia/-ío/-io	-y	historia/history geografía/geography fotografía/ photography biología/biology
Nouns and adjectives ending in consonant, add –o/a or -e		inteligente/intelligent tímido/timid estúpido/stupid experimento/ experiment clase/class física/physical uniforme/uniform estudiante/student
Adverbs ending in -mente	-ly	desafortunadamente/ unfortunately
verb forms ending in -ando or iendo	-ing	estudiando/studying

Page 14

① (a) i En el concurso de gimnasia no tuve <u>éxito</u> y salí en <u>último</u> lugar.

ii Mi amigo es una persona <u>sensible</u> y le <u>disgustan</u> las <u>discusiones</u> en el <u>patio</u>.

iii La comida del instituto es bastante <u>sana</u>, pero las <u>sopas</u> son <u>saladas</u> y por lo tanto siempre bebo un <u>vaso</u> de agua.

iv Mi profesora <u>envía</u> cartas a casa si no somos <u>educados</u>.

v No <u>recuerdo</u> dónde está la <u>parada</u> de autobús <u>escolar</u>.

vi Voy a <u>realizar</u> una <u>encuesta</u> para ver cuántas personas <u>asisten</u> a los clubs extraescolares.

b i In the gymnastics competition I wasn't successful and I came last.

ii My friend is a sensitive person and he is upset by arguments in the playground.

iii The food at school is quite healthy but the soups are salty and therefore I always drink a glass of water.

iv My teacher sends letters home if we are rude.

v I don't remember where the school bus stop is.

vi I'm going to carry out a survey about how many people attend the extracurricular activities.

2 **a** vi actual = current

b ii fábrica = factory

c ix bombero = firefighter

d i campo = countryside/field

e iii constiparse = to catch a cold

f x chocar = to crash

g iv una desgracia = misfortune

h viii embarazada = pregnant

a vii pariente = relative

Page 15

Exam-style question

1 every term

2 two years

3 playing with other people

4 to win a trophy

Page 16

Exam-style question

1 he started to get used to the differences between the two countries (look for 'acostumbrarme' = to get accustomed/used to, 'diferencias' = differences; don't be led astray by 'al principio' = at the beginning, not in principal or 'disgustaba' = upset, not disgusted)

2 that British pupils can't wear their own clothes/have to wear a uniform (look for 'curiosa' = curious/strange, 'alumnos' = alumni/pupils, and in the next sentence the mention of 'uniforme' = uniform. Careful with 'ropa' = clothes, not rope)

3 Any summary that conveys the point that on an exchange you learn about life in another country (look for 'recomiendo' = I recommend, 'diaria' = daily, 'costumbres' = customs)

Page 17

Page 10 Exam-style question

1 36.5%

2 girls

3 Victims are no longer silent. / Teachers are more aware of bullying.

Page 11 Exam-style question

1 they are not adequate

2 sports science

3 old labs

4 maths teacher

Unit 3

Page 19

1 Possible answers: desayunar, una cafetería, la barra, pedir, donuts, el camarero, tiene hambre

Page 20

1 | | |
|---|---|
| a menudo | frecuentemente |
| desafortunadamente | desgraciadamente |
| usar | utilizar |
| dar una vuelta | dar un paseo |
| divertido | entretenido |
| el ordenador | el portátil |
| el teléfono | el móvil |
| lo bueno de | la ventaja de |
| se puede | es posible |

2 **a** Se utilizan — Se usan,
gratuito — gratis

b se puede — es posible
el teléfono — el móvil
el portátil — el ordenador

c desgraciadamente — desafortunadamente

d Muchas veces — Frecuentemente
divertidos — entretenidos

Page 21

1 A d B c C a D b

2
	a	b
chatty	habladora	callada
we fight	nos peleamos	nos llevamos bien
optimistic	optimista	pesimista
responsible	responsable	irresponsable
friendly	simpático	antipático
patient	paciente	impaciente

c C, D, E, H

Page 22

1 **a** i leisure activities

ii weather

iii physical description

iv food

b i biografía, novelas, ciencia ficción, historias de vampiros

    ii hace mucho viento, hace sol, va a llover

    iii guapa, alta, delgada, pelo moreno, largo y rizado, ojos marrones

    iv ensalada, mariscos, gazpacho, pollo, gambas, postre, flan, helado, fruta

(2) a i transport and travel B

    ii sports and leisure activities A

  b Este modelo es el más _rápido_ con una velocidad máxima de _200 kilómetros por hora_. Además, es el más lujoso y más _cómodo_ de la nueva serie. Debajo de los _asientos de detrás_, hay un cajón especial para poner los portátiles, el monedero, los móviles o las cámaras.

    Acabamos de salir del _estadio_. ¡El _partido_ fue fantástico! Vamos a coger un taxi porque está lloviendo y hay muchísima gente haciendo cola para entrar al metro – incluyendo los hinchas del otro _equipo_, ¡todos de mal humor por la derrota!

(3) a a speed

  b a box

  c the supporters

  d the defeat

Page 23

Exam-style question

1 C

2 A

3 D

4 B

Page 24

Exam-style question

1 a good friend must be loyal

2 because he's funny and he makes her laugh

3 they are very different

4 Daniel

5 she likes reading science fiction while Daniel prefers stories about vampires

Page 25

Page 18 Exam-style question

1 I

2 A

3 H

4 G

5 F

Page 19 Exam-style question

1 B

2 B

3 C

4 A

5 B

Unit 4

Page 28

(1) a what

  b who

  c when

  d where

  e how much

  f how

  g which

  h why

(2) a a place

  b a choice

  c a person

  d a reason

  e a number

  f a time

  g an activity

(3) a and b

    i b (entradas)

    ii e (cinco)

    iii a (Sudamérica)

    iv f (tarde, mañana)

    v g (ir)

    vi c (hermano)

    vii d (porque)

Page 29

(1) a (work) actriz y cantante

  b (where, from) Londres

  c (how many, languages) 3: inglés, español, vasco

  d (part of Spain, father from) el país vasco, norte de España

  e (instrument) el acordeón

  f (TV series) Juego de tronos

(2) a She's an actress and a singer.

  b She's from London.

  c She speaks three languages.

  d Her father is from the Basque country in the north of Spain.

  e She plays the accordion.

  f She's appeared in _Game of Thrones_.

(3) A b

  B f

  C a

  D c

  E g

  F d

  G e

Page 30

1 **a** i es ideal para, porque hay música fantástica

ii lista de los grupos, sitios públicos, internet

iii festival, del 27 and 29 de abril

iv entrada, 65 euros, dormir

v no quieres llevar, organización, alquila, pocos euros

vi *Los Locos* y *Kaos Urbano*, más de 140 grupos

b i music lovers

ii posters

iii takes places

iv camping

v tent

vi are headlining

2 **a** decepcionante

b escalofriante

c impresionante

3 **a** The last episode wasn't as good as the previous ones so it was 'disappointing'.

b A horror film is likely to be 'frightening / chilling'.

c The recent novel has good characters and style, so it's 'impressive'.

Page 31

Exam-style question

1 Monday to Friday morning

2 Children older than 4

3 swim

4 Mondays

5 Children younger than 8

Page 32

1 Being healthier in the future.

2 Thirty minutes to an hour.

3 Avoiding obesity and depression; being disciplined; being able to work as part of a team, respect others and follow rules.

Page 33

Page 26 Exam-style question

1 E

2 F

3 B

4 A

Page 27 Exam-style question

1 B

2 B

3 A

4 A

5 C

Unit 5

Page 35

1 estoy – present

es – present

no hay … que hacer – present

es – present

tiene – present

voy a pasar – future

será – future

celebran – present

fui – past

estuve – past

voy a ir – future

Empieza – present

Page 36

1

pasado mañana	F	anoche	P	esta noche	F	ahora	N
anteayer	P	el julio pasado	P	mañana por la tarde	F	ayer	P
de momento	N	hace dos semanas	P	el lunes que viene	F	hoy	N
el mes próximo	F	en el porvenir	F	a partir de mañana	F	hace un siglo	P

2 **a** i todos los sábados

ii hace muchos años

iii De momento

iv La semana próxima

v Ahora, antes

vi a partir del sábado que viene

vii el mes pasado

b i N

ii F

iii P

iv F

v P

Page 37

1 **a** and **b**

Solía decir – imperfect

Están – present

tienes que llevar – present

ir de compras – infinitive

fui – preterite

cogí – preterite

no puedo resistir entrar – present

están – present

contestó – preterite

Debes ir – present

encontrarás – future

2 **a** Las tiendas abiertas

Una amiga nuestra solía decir:

— Están tan frías las tiendas que tienes que llevar
un abrigo para ir de compras. La última vez que fui
cogí un constipado, pero no puedo resistir entrar
en ellas porque están siempre abiertas.

— Pues buen remedio, un amigo le contestó.
"Debes ir solo los días de fiesta por la tarde y las
encontrarás cerradas."

b i N

ii P

iii N

iv F

Page 38

1 **a** Quise comprar unas botas nuevas para el invierno.
La zapatería estaba en la calle principal pero no la
encontraba. Pedí direcciones a un hombre y me
contestó; "No está abierta de momento, mejor ir a
los grandes almacenes". Tomé un autobús que me llevó
allí. Una dependienta me preguntó qué quería. Le
contesté que quería unas botas. "No tenemos muchas
en verano," ella me respondió. "¿Ves dónde están las
sandalias? Pues, las botas se encuentran a la derecha".

b
quise	José
estaba	shoe shop
encontraba	José
pedí	José
contestó	Man
está	shoe shop
tomé	José
llevó	bus
preguntó	shop assistant
quería	José
contesté	José
quería	José
tenemos	we
respondió	shop assistant
ves	José
están	sandals
se encuentran	boots

2 **a** Ana's father

b Pedro's mother

c the street plans

d I

e the bus

Page 39

Exam-style question

1 N

2 P

3 N

4 F

Page 40

Exam-style question

1 P

2 N

3 N

4 P

5 F

Page 41

Page 34 Exam-style question

1 Sunday

2 Alejandro

3 In the middle of the street

4 The boots were still OK (useful) / He didn't like to throw
anything away

Page 35 Exam-style question

1 N

2 F

3 P

4 F

Unit 6

Page 43

1 deduction

Page 44

1 Text a

☒ Contradicts the text, she normally stays at home,
but not always and not this coming New Year.

☒ Wrong, the question asks 'how' she is spending
New Year, not 'what' she does at New Year.

☒ Could work but ambiguous, she will be there at the
time.

✓ Correct answer

Text b

☒ Wrong, question is asking 'what' he likes to cook the most, not 'when' he likes to cook.

☒ Wrong, he cooks these among other things, but not the most.

☑ Correct answer

☒ Wrong, the text doesn't mention chips at all.

Page 45

① ⓐ Difficult to make a paella in the street for so many people.

ⓑ Because they were more spectacular.

ⓒ Huge figures of comic scenes and famous people

Page 46

① ⓐ en salas de toda España

ⓑ un precio reducido por entrada

ⓒ en las taquillas de los cines, y por internet

ⓓ medio millón más

ⓔ los partidos de semifinales

② ⓐ It's the biggest in Spain and lasts 3 days. The question is not about how long the festival lasts.

ⓑ They come from all over the world to demonstrate their skills. The question is not about what they have come to do.

ⓒ sports skills at the hands of the experts The question doesn't ask about who teaches in the workshops

③ ⓐ all over Spain

ⓑ reduced ticket price

ⓒ cinema box offices and online / over the internet

ⓓ half a million

ⓔ (Champions League semi-finals) football matches

Page 47

Exam-style question

1 the whole family

2 the first star

3 talk like humans / in human language

4 go to church

5 sweets and / or money

Page 48

Exam-style question

1 in his town ('en mi pueblo')

2 eating (so much) meat ('comer tanta carne')

3 eat less meat and more local products

Page 49

Page 42 Exam-style question

1 train station

2 friendly

3 French

4 two

5 lunch

Page 43 Exam-style question

1 He made her a card.

2 She loved it (more than all the other presents).

3 Any summary that conveys the point that you don't need to spend a lot of money on a present to give pleasure.

Unit 7

Page 52

① ⓐ P

ⓑ N

ⓒ P

ⓓ P

ⓔ N

ⓕ P

ⓖ N

ⓗ P

ⓘ N

ⓙ P

ⓚ P

ⓛ N

② A aprender – e to learn

B aburrirse – a to be bored

C ayudar – c to help

D ganar (dinero) – b to earn (money)

E mejorar – d to improve

F viajar – f to travel

③ ⓐ El sueldo es muy pero tienes que trabajar muchas horas.

ⓑ El horario es y lo bueno es que tienes los fines de semana libres.

ⓒ El jefe es bastante severo pero nos explica bien las tareas.

ⓓ El trabajo no era difícil pero llegó a ser.

ⓔ Lo mejor de las prácticas fue que. Fue una experiencia útil.

ⓕ Gané muy poco dinero pero mi nivel de español.

ⓖ El trabajo no era interesante. Fue una pérdida de tiempo.

Page 53

① ⓐ Creo que es importante aprender idiomas.

ⓑ Nuestros profesores piensan que vale la pena hacer prácticas laborables.

ⓒ En mi opinión, no es necesario pasar la aspiradora todos los días.

ⓓ Mi abuelo dice que no importa qué haces sino cómo lo haces.

ⓔ Para mí, lo más importante es hacer un trabajo útil.

② ⓐ una desventaja (trabajar en el extranjero; no hablar)

ⓑ vale la pena (puedes aprender mucho)

ⓒ desafortunadamente (Me gustaría; no saco buenas notas)

ⓓ una buena idea (los que hacen de canguro)

ⓔ Admiro (valientes; ayudan a la gente)

③ Creo que tengo mucha suerte porque tengo un trabajo que me encanta. Me chifla el deporte y soy profesor de educación física. Lo que más me gusta es ver cómo los chicos se divierten cuando hacen deporte y cómo aprenden a trabajar en equipo y llevarse bien con sus compañeros. Además, pienso que la actividad física ayuda a los jóvenes a estudiar mejor y a tener más confianza en sí mismos. El aspecto negativo es que siempre hay algunos estudiantes que no quieren trabajar, pero afortunadamente, son una minoría.

Page 54

① ⓐ ¿En qué día Pablo planea su viaje a la entrevista?

Which two entries refer to going somewhere?	Which of the two entries talks about going shopping?	The answer to the question is:
Sábado + martes	sábado	martes

ⓑ ¿En qué día Pablo se informará sobre la compañía?

Which two entries refer to finding information?	Which of the two entries talks about transport information?	The answer to the question is:
Domingo + martes	martes	domingo

ⓒ ¿En qué día Pablo pensará en preguntas que puede usar en la entrevista?

Which two entries refer to questions?	Which of the two entries talks about questions likely to be asked at interview?	The answer to the question is:
Lunes + miércoles	miércoles	lunes

Page 55

Exam-style question

1 No; Taking a gap year is relatively new in Spain.

2 She improved her English. / She became more independent and responsible.

3 Taking a gap year enables students to find out about other cultures and to learn languages. It also helps them to improve their communication skills, to be more adaptable, to work as part of a team and to be more open-minded.

Page 56

Exam-style question

1 working as a shop assistant and selling clothes

2 to fill in for permanent staff who are away on holiday

3 you get discounts on clothes

4 teenagers who are at least 16

5 you don't get paid much

Page 57

Page 50 Exam-style question

1 D

2 C

3 A

4 B

5 E

Page 51 Exam-style question

1 B

2 B

3 A

4 C

5 A

6 C

Unit 8

Page 59

① ⓐ They took part more of 50 people.

ⓑ It was quite cold and it was windy, but we had a good time.

ⓒ Afterwards, we all had breakfast in the bar of the village.

ⓓ We are going to do the race again the year coming.

Page 60

① ⓐ Cycling is very popular now.

ⓑ We went on a trip to the mountains two weeks ago. (hace dos semanas)

ⓒ In the big cities, there are too many homeless people. (demasiada)

ⓓ Drinking too much alcohol is quite a serious problem. (bastante)

② ⓐ Me encanta el deporte y normalmente practico algún deporte casi todos los días. Casi nunca veo la tele porque es aburrido, pero hace poco vi un campeonato de atletismo en que una atleta de mi region ganó una medalla. Fue muy emocionante. El año que viene me gustaría participar en un triatlón.

ⓑ *I love sport and I usually do some kind of sport nearly every day. I hardly ever watch TV because it's boring, but a little while ago, I watched an*

athletics championship in which an athlete from my area won a medal. It was very exciting. I would like to take part in a triathlon next year.

Page 61

1

a I think the most worrying problem is ~~the~~ climate change.

b We must protect the ~~tropical~~ forests.

c We should encourage ~~to~~ everyone to recycle more.

d I go to ~~the~~ school by bike or on foot every day.

e ~~The pollution of the~~ air in ~~the~~ big cities is a serious problem. Air pollution is a serious problem in big cities.

f ~~The car of~~ my father ~~is electric.~~ My father's car is electric.

2

a I live in an industrial city to the north of Barcelona.

b The environmental problem that worries me most is air pollution.

c There are too many cars and lorries in the city centre.

d We should use public transport or go on foot.

e We must inform the public about the importance of looking after the environment.

Page 62

1

a En casa hacemos todo lo posible para ahorrar energía. En invierno, sólo usamos la calefacción cuando hace mucho frío. En verano, cerramos las cortinas y las persianas durante el día y la casa se queda fresca por dentro. De esta manera, sólo usamos los ventiladores cuando hace mucho calor. Además, tenemos placas solares en el tejado para calentar el agua.

b
i	heating	We only use it when it's cold.
ii	blinds	We keep them closed to keep the house cool.
iii	radiators	We only use them when it's very hot.
iv	solar panels	They heat the water.
v	roof	Solar panels are usually on the roof.

2

a Voy a comer más ensalada, verduras y fruta.

I'm going to eat more salad, ~~leaves~~ and fruit. (vegetables)

b Me gustan las manzanas pero no me gustan las peras.

I like apples but I don't like ~~hot dogs.~~ (pears)

c Vivimos en un barrio en las afueras de la ciudad y hay mucho tráfico.

We live in a ~~bar~~ in the outskirts of the city and there is a lot of traffic. (neighbourhood)

d Hay que apagar las luces para ahorrar energía.

We must switch ~~on~~ the lights to save energy. (off)

Page 63

Exam-style question

I think paralympic athletes are good role models for children and young people because they fight to overcome many difficulties. Also, I think it's worthwhile taking part in charity events. Recently, I volunteered at a cycle race in my area that raised money for homeless people. It was a very positive experience.

Page 64

Exam-style question

Two months ago, I changed my job and now I haven't got time to go to the gym nor the swimming pool. To relax, I started smoking but now I need to change my routine to have a healthy lifestyle. I think that, from Monday to Friday, I'm going to get up earlier to go running before going to the office. I'm going to change my diet and eat more salad, vegetables and fruit. In addition, I'm going to stop smoking.

Page 65

Page 58 Exam-style question

I live in a small town in the north of Spain. I like swimming and I like gymastics. Last year, I went on holiday to France with my parents, my sister, my uncle and aunt and my cousins. We went by car and it was quite a long journey but we had a great time. This year, I'm going (/ I will go) to a summer camp in the mountains with my sister.

Page 59 Exam-style question

In February, we organised a bike race in my village. More than 50 people took part. It was quite cold and windy but, despite the bad weather, we had a good time. Afterwards we all had breakfast in the village bar. We're going to the race again next year.

Unit 9

Page 68

1

a Protege tu planeta

Ves los consejos para cuidar el medio ambiente.

b Un año académico en Canadá

Lee sobre la experiencia de un estudiante español en el extranjero.

c Manolito Gafotas by Elvira Lindo

Read the text about Manolito's day out in Madrid with his grandfather.

d ¿Se puede vivir sin el móvil?

Ves este artículo sobre cómo la tecnología móvil nos cambia la vida.

2

a i night walk

ii lived with

iii there's no signal

b i The heading mentions a sports event and the text in Spanish mentions luz de la luna or 'moonlight'.

ii The highlighted word conviví con suggests it's meaning is related to vivir 'to live'

iii The heading mentions mobile technology, and the text in Spanish mentions cobertura which is likely a cognate for 'coverage' which suggests it's referring to mobile signal.

Page 69

1

a (La canción,) *Despacito*, ha sido el (número uno) en las listas de éxito en más de ochenta países del mundo. A

b El guión de (la película) estaba (mal escrito,) pero por lo menos los actores eran buenos. D

c Fuimos a un partido en el Camp Nou y el ambiente (en el estadio era fantástico.) D

d Para ir a la boda de mi prima, tuve que (llevar traje y corbata). A

e No ha sido (una serie de televisión) de alta calidad, pero ha sido muy entretenida. E

f (La música) de las bandas sonoras de (Gladiador y El Señor de los Anillos) ha llegado a ser (música clásica) (de cine). A

g Según (una encuesta) reciente, (60% de los españoles) no ha leído *El Quijote*. C

2

a record charts

b script

c atmosphere

d wedding

e entertaining

f soundtracks

g according to

Page 70

1

a interactuar = interact, convivir = live with, malgastarás / malgastar = waste, imposible = imposible

b prever = forsee, malentender = misunderstand, impaciente = impatient

c desafortunadamente = unfortunately, anteayer = the day before yesterday, incapaz = incapable

2

a panadero = occupation = baker, hablador = verb → adjective = talkative, simpaticón = augmentative = very friendly, panadería = shop = bakery, callecita = diminutive = little street, encantadora = verb to adjective = charming, frecuentemente = adjective → adverb = frequently

b lavadora = verb → noun = washing machine, secador = verb → noun = (hair) dryer, aspiradora = verb → noun = vacuum cleaner, comedor = verb → place = dining room

c voluntario = "-ary" = voluntary, medioambiental = noun → adjective = enviromental

3 subalimentación = alimento = nourishment

desordenadamente = orden = disorderly

agrandamiento = grande = enlargement

aconsejar = consejo = advise

entremetido = meter = meddling, intruding

desilusionante = ilusión = disappointing

Page 71

Exam-style question

1 Helps the most needy in Havana

2 they aren't easy to get in Cuba

3 It supports people with donated items and help from volunteers

4 He didn't have a wheel chair

5 The generosity of the Cuban people

Page 72

Exam-style question

1 Loved ones far away

2 They work more than 14 hours per day

3 Instead of going to school they beg in the streets

4 They are things you don't see in the media.

5 Back packers communicate in English.

Page 73

Page 66 Exam-style question

1 In the 1940s

2 14

3 she looked after her house and her children

4 they don't show respect

5 clothes for the children

Page 67 Exam-style question

1 B

2 A

3 D

4 C

5 A

Notes